Ancient Wisdom When All Else Fails

A NEW TRANSLATION
& INTERPRETIVE
PARAPHRASE

ECCLESIASTES

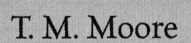

T. M. Moore

InterVarsity Press
Downers Grove, Illinois

InterVarsity Press
P.O. Box 1400, Downers Grove, IL 60515-1426
World Wide Web: www.ivpress.com
E-mail: mail@ivpress.com

InterVarsity Press® is the book-publishing division of InterVarsity Christian Fellowship/USA®, a student movement active on campus at hundreds of universities, colleges and schools of nursing in the United States of America, and a member movement of the International Fellowship of Evangelical Students. For information about local and regional activities, write Public Relations Dept., InterVarsity Christian Fellowship/USA, 6400 Schroeder Rd., P.O. Box 7895, Madison, WI 53707-7895.

Unless otherwise indicated, all Scripture quotations are the author's translation.

Cover illustration: Roberta Polfus

ISBN 0-8308-2111-2

Printed in the United States of America ∞

Library of Congress Cataloging-in-Publication Data

Bible. O.T. Ecclesiastes. English. Moore. 2001.
    Ecclesiastes: ancient wisdom when all else fails: a new translation & interpretive
paraphrase/T.M. Moore.
        p. cm.
    Includes bibliographical references.
    ISBN 0-8308-2111-2 (cloth: alk. paper)
    1. Bible. O.T. Ecclesiastes—Paraphrases, English. I. Moore, T. M., 1947-II. Title.
BS1473 2001
223'.805209—dc21   00-054450

19	18	17	16	15	14	13	12	11	10	9	8	7	6	5	4	3	2	1
17	16	15	14	13	12	11	10	09	08	07	06	05	04	03	02	01

For George and Dorothy Moore

In the wisdom of God

CONTENTS

Acknowledgments

Steve Kowit, for permission to quote Steve Kowit, "Notice," in A Book of Luminous Things, ed. Czeslaw Milosz (New York: Harcourt Brace, 1996).

Joyce Sutphen, for permission to quote Joyce Sutphen, "Into Thin Air," Poetry, July 1999.

Introduction

My love for Ecclesiastes goes back thirty years, to when I first read it as a college student. I remember being struck by the relevance of its questions—about the fleeting nature of materialism, fame and self-promotion, and about the meaning of human life in the larger scheme of things—as well as the honesty and urgency of the writing. At the same time I was baffled by its mysterious images and analogies and the curious way it argues for transcendence. I was utterly convinced of the truth of its conclusions, although I cannot say I understood them fully at that time (or, indeed, even now).

Over the years I have meditated on, studied, preached and taught this book to church members and seminary students and have always found its approach and message a challenge to people from every walk of life. Each time I have studied or taught Ecclesiastes I have become more convinced of the importance of this book for our times. In offering the examination of Ecclesiastes contained in the pages that follow, I hope readers will take a new look at the old wisdom with which this book confronts us, and discover the urgent and wonderful truths that Solomon unfolds for our consideration.

Authorship

Many commentators have argued for an author or authors other than the one claimed in the book itself, primarily on the basis of linguistic considerations. The presence of some Aramaic words, which must have come from beyond the time of Solomon, and the change of perspective—from third person in the introduction to first person throughout the body of text, and then back to third person again at the end—lead many commentators to look beyond the obvious claims of the book and to posit an author other than Solomon.

But it is possible to account for these phenomena without abandoning Solomonic authorship. It is quite possible that Ecclesiastes, like other biblical books (cf. Prov 25:1), was subjected to later editorializing or updating by scribes eager to preserve and clarify the message of this difficult book for their own day. Certainly it was copied by later generations, as the many textual variants indicate. Such updating and copying could account for the occasional later word that appears.

It is also possible that an introduction and conclusion was tacked on by one or more of these later editors, as seems to be the case with the Gospel of Mark. The scribes who prepared the version of Ecclesiastes that appears in the Hebrew canon may have considered such additional material perfectly legitimate, a part of the inspired text.

Alternately, Solomon himself may well, for reasons known only to him, have chosen to use the third person to open and close his book; after all, David, his father, used the third person—referring to himself as "the king"—in many of his psalms.

Thus I have not been persuaded by the arguments for non-Solomonic authorship. I take a traditional approach to this question, following several of the commentators cited in the notes to the text (especially Bridges, Kaiser and Kelley). Solomon, who wandered from God during a prosperous period of life, only to return to him later, is writing this book as a final testament to his son Rehoboam, in whom he must have seen some of the same tendencies that had led him into a life of vanity. Solomon appears to have come to his senses at the end of his days and is urgent to warn his son—and all subsequent readers—not to fall into the mistakes he did. Too late for Rehoboam, who had already made up his mind to use the throne of Israel for his personal aggrandizement (1 Kings 12:1-14). Many of the details of the text can be connected with the life and work of Solomon. So as I show in the notes to chapter 1, the strong claim of Solomonic authorship should be taken seriously.

Argument

Solomon's purpose is to warn his son—and subsequent readers—away from self-centeredness and life apart from God by recalling the many ways that he attempted to find meaning and happiness during his own period of straying from God, and by showing the folly of every such course of life. He recounts his initial intention to find the wisdom he would need in order to serve the nation of Israel as a responsible king. Though he began well, he drifted from that course into self-indulgence and faithlessness, flitting from one diversion to another, hoping to find some lasting happiness in the things of this life. He details his many works and activities, none of which brought him any peace or lasting satisfaction, and reflects on them in the light of his return to the Lord in old age. The book stands as a warning to those who hope to make sense out of their lives apart from God, calling them to use sound reason and common sense, to learn to be content with what God gives and to live in gratitude before him. Made in the image of God—with "eternity in their hearts" (Eccles 3:11)—we are advised to resist the temptation to live apart from God. Instead, taking what God gives us, we should give ourselves entirely to knowing, loving and serving him—the only sensible way to find full and abundant life.

This interpretation of the purpose of Ecclesiastes largely hangs on one's understanding of the phrases "under the heavens" and "under the sun." Most—but not all—commentators[a] take these phrases as essentially equivalent, merely different ways of saying the same thing. I see them instead as opposing phrases, used throughout the book to set the discussion either in an earthbound or in a God-oriented frame of reference (see note d to chapter 1).

Three reasons drive me to this judgment. First, these phrases are not used with equality in Ecclesiastes. "Under the heavens" occurs only twice—in 1:13 and 3:1—while "under the sun" occurs no fewer than twenty-three times. If they were in fact equivalent phrases, one might expect a more equal use of the two. Solomon seems to be deliberate and judicious in his use of them, preferring "under the sun" to "under the heavens" in order to drive home his argument about the futility of life apart from God.

Second, the context in which the phrases are used indicates a difference in their purposes. "Under the heavens" is used at the beginning of Solomon's search for wisdom, after he had asked the Lord for this great gift and begun the process of preparing himself for his calling as king (Eccles 1:13; compare 2 Chron 1:8-12). Here, at the beginning of his reign, Solomon resolved to serve the nation according to the wisdom of God and set himself a course of discovering and discerning that wisdom as fully as he could. His outlook was grounded in faith and obedience, his prospects were bright, and his hopes were high. The only other place in Ecclesiastes where "under the heavens" occurs is 3:1. In this section—3:1-15—Solomon is reflecting, at the end of his life, on the conclusions that should be drawn from all his wandering and seeking. He seems to be musing on the results of his experience and asserting that everything in the world has its own place when seen with the eye of faith and from God's perspective, appearances to the contrary notwithstanding.[b] Thus the phrase "under the heavens" is used only in contexts in which proper, heaven-oriented motivations, aspirations and conclusions are in view.

"Under the sun," on the other hand, always occurs in a context marked by futility, frustration, vanity and "chasing after the wind." And although Solomon intends his readers to understand that life under the sun is a gift from God and should be received and enjoyed as such, he is at pains to show us that life *looked at from that perspective alone* never quite seems to make sense. The phrase "under the sun" repeatedly punctuates the futility and meaninglessness of life lived only for self and the moment, without gratitude to or regard for God and his ways.

Finally, the distribution of these phrases in Ecclesiastes suggests a difference in their meaning. "Under the heavens" comes only at the beginning of the book, in chapters 1 and 3, when Solomon is recalling his noble beginnings and reflecting on the conclusions to be drawn from his long years of wandering and seeking, while "under the sun" is distributed liberally throughout the book. Since the vast bulk of the text of Ecclesiastes is given to what many people might regard as a depressing, discouraging argument, it would make sense to find this earthbound referent serving as a peg for Solomon's comments throughout his essay as he works through his observations and deliberations about the meaning and purpose of life.

I should mention a final, perhaps more subjective reason that I see a difference between these phrases. Throughout my years of studying and teaching Ecclesiastes this reading of these phrases has helped me to keep the overall argument of the book in view and to make sense of what can otherwise seem to be uncertain, indecipherable ramblings. If we keep in mind, in those contexts where "under the sun" is being used, that Solomon is arguing against a merely earthbound approach to life—whether materialistic, hedonistic or relativistic—and that he often employs irony, diatribe and *reductio ad absurdum* arguments to make his point, his often confusing and seemingly contradictory statements can be held in tension and made to work together for a proper understanding of these passages in their larger context.

Structure

Ecclesiastes does not lend itself to easy outlining. Part biography, part poetry, part proverbs and wisdom statements, and part diatribe, it invites us to savor its various chapters as separate points in an overall argument for transcendent living. The chapter divisions in this book follow those in Ecclesiastes, attempting to show how each section makes its particular contribution to the argument of the book as a whole. This is not necessarily a logical approach to the book, but it seems to work well for the purposes of group or individual study. For a more logical breakdown of the contents of Ecclesiastes, see the outlines proposed in various commentaries cited.

Format of This Book

This book consists of a new translation of Ecclesiastes, an interpretive paraphrase, a study guide and detailed analytical notes. The translation was necessary for my own process of study and in order to bring more consistency to the overall argument of the text.

The most curious aspect of the book will be the rhyming paraphrase, yet this is not a new approach to biblical commentary. As far back as Ephraem the Syrian (c. 306-373) and Prudentius (348-c. 410), biblical commentators have employed verse forms to help their readers gain a new perspective on what for many of them would have been familiar terrain. In modern times, John Milton (1608-1674) used blank verse (unrhymed iambic pentameter) in his biblical epics on the Fall, Samson and redemption. The verse form employed in this book is heroic couplets and is intended not so much to comment on the text as to elucidate its teaching through a dramatic elaboration of the argument of each chapter.

The study guide can be used by individuals or groups in order to explore the argument of Ecclesiastes more fully and draw out contemporary applications of this timely book of Scripture. Students of Ecclesiastes should find the analytical notes helpful for comparing translations as well as the work of modern commentators.

How to Use This Book

Study of each chapter of Ecclesiastes may begin with a reading of the translation, comparing the work in this book with your own preferred version of Scripture. In the translation words that appear in roman type are not in the actual Hebrew text but are supplied to make sense of the context. This is standard translation procedure. The analytical notes accompanying the translation will help to tease out Solomon's argument, clarify difficult readings of the Hebrew text and allow the student to see how other commentators have dealt with the passage. Note that not all the analytical notes relate to the translation; some are attached to the interpretive paraphrase and should be read in that context.

Then read the interpretive paraphrase, keeping one eye on the biblical text and allowing the analytical notes to the paraphrase to provide further explanations and clarifications. I have used bold text in the paraphrase to indicate where each verse of a chapter begins, and the typesetters have graciously worked, as far as possible, to keep the translation and the interpretive paraphrase alongside each other on a verse-by-verse basis.

Finally, use the study questions for personal or group study and discussion and for personal application. There is a lesson for each chapter of Ecclesiastes, together with an introductory lesson to set the stage for your study of this book. (Since this introductory lesson does not require this book, or even having read Ecclesiastes, it can give study leaders an opportunity to pass out books and begin with a group discussion designed to set the stage for the remaining lessons.) The thirteen lessons in the study guide make it suitable for a Sunday school quarter, a Bible study group subject, or even to pace a college or seminary semester. Writing out answers to the each of the questions will help to firm up your conclusions and applications and help you get the most out of the study of Ecclesiastes.

Each study begins and ends with quotations from commentators cited throughout this book. The quotes are intended to help set the tone and theme and to focus on the primary points to be emphasized in each lesson. Students should meditate on the opening quote before beginning to respond to study questions and then use the concluding quotes to draw the lesson to a focused conclusion.

There are five sections of questions for each lesson. Whether you are studying individually or leading a group through these studies, it works best to read all the questions in a section first—for example, all the questions in section one—and then go back and answer each question one at a time. If you are leading a group, try to allow as many people as possible to respond to questions, and invite group members to comment helpfully on one another's responses. Summarize what group members have shared as you conclude each section. After you have answered all the questions in one section, move on to the next section and do the same, until you have worked through all the questions in the lesson. Use the concluding quotes as an opportunity for further individual or group reflection on the primary themes.

Purpose of This Book

My purpose in this book is to share the insights and understandings I have acquired over the years from the study of Ecclesiastes and to enable students to gain as much benefit as possible from their own study of this ancient book. Readers should linger over Solomon's arguments, reflecting on how his views on any subject—relationships, work, civil government, the meaning of life—may intersect with or challenge their own. Let *Ecclesiastes* lead you to examine your worldview—the ideas you hold about what is important in life, what has value and will last—as well as to reflect on the worldviews of those around you. Consider Solomon's experience in the light of your own, and think about how your life would be different if faith in God guided your attitudes, decisions and activities more consistently.

This book will have accomplished its purpose if its readers come to see that life without God is truly "vanity of vanities," a frustrating and disappointing "chasing after the wind," and if they discover a renewed determination to know the One who brought Solomon to his senses and who is still doing the same today.

I should like to express my gratitude to Andy Le Peau, the staff at InterVarsity Press and the various readers of early drafts of this text. Their help and encouragement have been indispensable to the successful conclusion of this project.

May the joy of knowing the Lord be yours as it was Solomon's and has been mine, along with countless others throughout the ages.

CHASING
THE WIND

I

At the end of his life,
Solomon reflects on his purpose and pursuits,
recalling the futility and frustration
he encountered
when he lost his way.

1 The words of the Worship Leader,ᵃ the son of David, king in Jerusalem:

THIS is my story, I who on the day
when God Almighty in that awful way
came down and filled his temple, stood before
his people, amid the fire and smoke, and wore
the robes of Worship Leader. I was king,
the son of David, ruling everything
and everyone in Jerusalem, that great
and glorious city: Hear what I relate:

2 "Utterly meaningless!" says the Worship Leader. "Utterly meaningless; everything is meaningless!"ᵇ

HOW vain, how meaningless it seemed to me;
all I had known and done was vanity!
No lasting peace or purpose could I find
to offer rest to body, soul or mind.

3 What profit does a man have from all his work at which he labors under the sun?ᶜ

WHAT does a man retain beyond the grave
from all the work in which he, like a slave,
consumes his days, as though this earthly life
were all there is? What's left from all this strife
and struggle?ᵈ

4 Each generation comes and goes, but the earth continues unchanged.ᵉ

EVERY age is just the same:
the generations come and go, the names
of some we know, but most are strangers to
us; countless, faceless men and women do
what they must do to carry on. They come
and go and scarcely leave a mark. The dumbᶠ
earth where they waste their futile days
is unaffected by their hapless ways.ᵍ

5 Also, *the sun rises and the sun sets; then it hastens*[h] *to its place and rises there* again.

I thought, Perhaps some answer lies within
the patterns of creation? The sun and wind,
the rains and seas—might not they yield to me
some secret insights that will let me be
at peace? The sun arises, sets and then
arises and completes its course again.

6 *The winds pursue their circuits too; from north to south and south to north they go, turning and returning on their daily course.*

THE winds their circuits ride as well, from north
to south and south to north. What is that worth?
They go upon their circuit day by day,
yet naught of truth or wisdom do they say.

7 *All the rivers flow to the sea, but the sea is not full; the waters return to the places from which they flowed.*

THE rivers flow into the sea, but it
does not fill up; indeed, it seems to spit
its contents to the clouds again, which bring
them back once more to where the rivers spring
to life and start their mindless march unto
the sea again. What lasting wisdom, true
perspective, purpose or understanding here
can I discern to give me hope or cheer?

8 *Everything is exhausting;*[i] *who can make sense of it all?*[j] *The eye cannot get enough of seeing, and the ear is not satisfied*[k] *with the things that it hears.*

SUCH contemplations wore me out, I do
confess. I know of no one living who
can sort it out or make sense of it all.
We read and study until our eyes must fall
to sleeping; listen though we may, we can
not hear enough to slake the thirst of man
for lasting truth.

9 It seems that *everything that is is merely a repetition of what has come before; whatever has been done in the past is what will be done* tomorrow as well. Nothing has changed, *there is nothing new under the sun.*[l]
10 Is *there something concerning which someone might say, "See*

                IT seemed (to me at least)
that what I'd hoped would be a sumptuous feast
of every sort of food to satisfy
my intellectual curiosity
was but a diet bland, unchanging. Life
was merely empty repetition, rife
with much activity, but nothing new.
O spare me, please! What makes you think that
  you

this—this is new"? It has already been around before our time, in fact, forever.

know more than I? All right then, show me, if
you can, just one new thing. I would not miff,
provoke or anger you, but I will tell
you plain: Whatever it is, they knew it well
in other generations, just as you.[m]
Believe me when I say there's nothing new.

11 We have learned nothing from the past;[n] indeed we scarcely even remember the things that previous generations have accomplished. And those who come after us will not be remembered by those who come after them.

THE past has taught us nothing. We forget
what's gone before, content to merely let
the lessons of the past escape our view.
Be sure the same fate waits for us; we too
will be ignored, forgotten in the dust
of history's mindless march. Do not distrust
my words: If all there is to this sad life
is work and study, consternation, strife
and then the grave, then all is vanity.[o]

12 I, the Worship Leader, have been[p] king over Israel in Jerusalem.[q] 13 I resolved[r] to inquire and investigate, as wisely as I could, everything that has been done under the heavens. This is a difficult matter[s] which God has given to the children of humankind to busy[t] and afflict them.

MY search began when I was king. For me,
the Worship Leader, it was not enough
to rule Jerusalem. **I** set a tough
course for myself, determining to learn
all that I could, so that I might discern
the truth of things, might see and understand
the whole of life as God intends for man
to do. This is no easy task, it's true,
but God on high has made us to pursue
this arduous work of wisdom, that we might
both please and honor him and find delight
in living in his presence.[u]

14 I have seen everything that has been done under the sun,[v] and listen: All of it is utterly meaningless. It makes no sense from that perspective, and amounts to chasing the wind.

IT was not
to be, however—not for me, who ought
to have known what happens when folks turn away
from God.[w] I could not be content to stay
within the orbit of his love. Instead
I set a course—but now I am ahead
of where I meant to be. Suffice it here
to say that if this earthly life is dear
to us above all else, that is, if we

deny heaven's claims upon our lives and see
ourselves as beings of this space in time
and nothing more, then neither things sublime
nor silly will cohere or satisfy.
I've tried it all, my son, I will deny
it not. And it is vain, I tell you, *vain!*
Like feeding[x] on the wind.[y]

*15 What is crooked cannot be
made straight, and what is lacking cannot be provided.[z]*

    THE awful pain
that comes when justice fails cannot be soothed
when lasting norms of right and good and truth
are all denied.[aa] And who will share their goods
with those less fortunate, although they should?[bb]

*16 I said to myself, Look, I have
become great and have increased
wisdom more than all those who
ruled before me in Jerusalem; and
my mind[cc] has considered tremen-
dous amounts of wisdom and
knowledge.*

I pondered my condition: What went wrong?
If I have learned so much and grown so strong
and wise, much more than any others who
have ruled this land before me, should I rue
this life as now I do? I'd seen and heard
as much as any man; and yet no word
of lasting truth had I prevailed to find.

*17 I had[dd] set my mind to know
wisdom, and to know foolishness
and madness as well; yet this has
proved to be[ee] nothing more than
chasing the wind.*

I'D dedicated all my strength of mind
to learn the wisdom of the ages. And
if truth be told, I came to understand
the ways of folly, even madness too,
along the way. But none of it would do
me any good. It was a feeding on
the wind, and nothing more.[ff]

*18 For much wisdom brings
much grief[gg] as well, and adding
knowledge adds pain.*

      FOR wisdom won
by ever so much striving, has a dark
side to it, since it sets into such stark
relief the grief of fools, the sadness of
oppressed and lonely people, and the love
of self that frustrates every noble plan
and vaunted scheme. I've come to understand
this well, my son; believe me when I tell
you, this way makes of life an earthly hell.[hh]

HATING LIFE

II

In more detail, Solomon reflects
on his course of life "under the sun,"
all his accomplishments and achievements,
and expresses disdain
for the futility of it all apart from God.

1 I said to myself, I will anoint myself with good times.[a] *But listen, this also is meaningless.*

2 I concluded that laughter and merriment for their own sakes *were madness. What did they accomplish* to help me find lasting meaning and purpose in life?

3 I resolved to cheer my body with wine, still seeking after wisdom, mind you,[b] *and to lay hold on revelry in order to see whether this*[c] *might yield the good I was seeking. Perhaps, since life is so short, folly and revelry might be the meaning of it all?*[d] *But no.*

4 I devoted myself[e] *to my work,* greatly increasing my holdings and my contributions to the public weal.[g] *I built houses and planted vineyards for myself.*

I was not at it very long, this quest
for understanding, when I thought it best
to take a break from study. Too much work
without some fun and games, you know, can irk
and bore beyond belief. I sought relief
in merriment, if I may but be brief.
We had some raucous times, to say the least,
but there was no more substance in this feast
of pleasure than there was in wisdom. All
was vain and meaningless, as I recall.

OH, there was great diversion, to be sure;
and I will not deny the strong allure
of merely having fun. BUT I was on
a larger quest than mere diversion, one
that haunted me, yes, even as I drank
myself to madness and indulged in rank
debauchery. In quieter moments I'd
reflect that merriment was on the side
of raw stupidity; what had I gained
through all of this? I saw that it was vain.
Though life is short and some might think that this
way lies the meaning of it all, they miss
the point, so I have seen.

ENOUGH of that;[f]
I dove back into work again. Here's what
I did: I set about to build for my
indulgence, houses, vineyards, GARDENS by
the score, replete with luscious fruit trees for

5 I made gardens and parks for myself and planted in them all kinds of fruit trees.
6 I constructed pools and reservoirs for myself, so that I could irrigate a forest of growing trees.
7 I acquired manservants and female slaves, as well as those born to me in my home. My herds and flocks were greater than all those who preceded me in Jerusalem.
8 I gathered to myself treasures of silver and gold, gifts from the kings and provinces that fell within the scope of my power.[h] I made sure to have plenty of men and women singers available to please me with song, and I did not deny myself the pleasure that all men seek— many lovers and concubines.[i]

9 Thus I became great and more powerful than all those who were before me in Jerusalem. What's more, I managed to maintain my wisdom through all this.[j]

10 I did not withhold from myself anything that my eyes desired; nor did I fail to indulge in any merriment that my heart craved. Moreover, I took great delight in all my labors and found them to be enormously satisfying.
11Thus I surveyed all that I had done and all that my hands had

my every taste. **I** built great reservoirs
and shining pools to suit my fancy and
to irrigate my growing forest stand
of precious trees.

　　　O F course, I'd need a staff
of servants to attend this all, the half
of which I have not told, and filled my home
and grounds with men and women whom I owned
just like the cattle and the flocks that I
increased beyond what anyone could buy
or had ever owned before me. **WEALTH** just
　　seemed
to flow to me! More wealth than I had dreamed
I'd ever know—the treasures of the lands
around Jerusalem came into my hands
in ever greater measure. What to do
with such a treasure? I determined to
surfeit my house with music. So I bought
great choirs of singers, men, of course, and not
a few young women too, a few of whom
—well, let's be honest—many who my room
and bed enjoyed. Come now, you'd do the same
if you possessed my wealth and power and fame!
YES, I became by far the greatest man
who ever lived within this city. And
you must believe me, all the while I told
myself it was for wisdom that I sold
my soul to self-indulgence of the sort
I have described.

　　　SO herewith my report:
I'd done it all, the fun and games as much
as I desired, and revelry of such
a sort you've only dreamed about. Besides
all that I'd known success and fortune. I'd
discovered these could satisfy one's soul
as much as any merriment. **BUT** oh,
what's left when all these vain pursuits are done?
What do I have to show for all that fun,

accomplished—all that revelry and all those great and beautiful works. And listen to me: All of it was meaningless and chasing the wind! As ends in themselves,[k] they yielded no lasting profit, no sense of meaning or purpose to my life.

for all that wealth, success and fame that I had worked so hard to gain? My sad reply is simple: Nothing. There is nothing left from all these vanities. I was bereft of any lasting good, of anything of meaning that might have the power to bring me any closer to the knowledge of what life was all about. Those things I'd loved so much, had given so much energy and time to, in the end abandoned me and left me feeding on the wind.[1]

12 I took some time to reflect on all this—on wisdom and madness and folly. I felt an obligation to those who would come after me, for what will they[m] be able to do more than I? 13 Of course, I saw that wisdom was more valuable by far than folly. It makes more sense to pursue the course of wisdom than to waste one's life in revelry and merriment. This was as clear as night and day to me. 14 The wise person leads with the mind,[n] taking a thoughtful approach to life. One who lives only for revelry doesn't think about anything except having fun. That person doesn't have a clue about things that really matter.[o] And yet I reflected on this one thing: The same fate befalls both these persons. In the end, they lie together in the grave!

I took some time to think on this and write this book. I wanted to reflect and to compare, for any after me who just might care to read my thoughts, the merits of the course of wisdom and of folly. Which is worse? Which better? AND of course, I came to see that wisdom far exceeded revelry; for, after all, the wise man thinks about his every action, how it might play out and whom it might affect, what benefit he might expect to realize from it, and so forth. BUT the fool cares not to use his brain; indeed, he often will refuse to take the course he knows is best if that will take him from his quest for pleasure. What cares he of things profound or things sublime? He has no inclination, has no time for such vain speculations. He subsists on fun and games and heartily resists whatever would dissuade him from his course. Oh, it is clear his way of life is worse by far than what the wise man chooses. Still, I contemplated this one thing: How will the life of each conclude? For it is clear one fate awaits them both, the dark, dank, drear defeat of death.

15 *So I pondered: If the fool's fate and mine are the same, then why have I worked so hard to be wise? Why all this study? this hard work? this arduous quest for some lasting meaning to my life? So I concluded that this also, this trying to make sense of it all, is meaningless.*

THIS rattled me. Oh how
I battled in my mind that I might know
why this should be! And more than that, since this
is so, then why choose one and just dismiss
the other?[p] More specific, what have I
determined on this quest for wisdom? Why
devote so many hours to study, and
why work so hard to try to understand
the meaning of it all, if in the end
I'll simply lie beside the fool and spend
eternity with him devouring dust?
So I concluded all this study must
be nothing more than vanity.

16 *For the wise person will not be remembered any more than the fool in the days to come. They will both be forgotten together. So the wise person and the fool die together, both in body and in the memories of those who come after them.[q]*

        THE days
to come will not recall either the ways
of fools or wise men. Both of them shall be
forgotten—yes, the foolish man and me!
Our bodies seek the dust of death and see
its shroud together for eternity.
We die as well within the memory
of all who follow after. Vanity!
What vanity, I tell you!

17 *And so I hated life! For all the work that had been accomplished under the sun was evil to me. It was all vanity and chasing the wind.*

        SO I came
to hate my life—my wealth, my works, my fame
and everything that I had done to find
some sense of purpose and some peace of mind.
I wanted life to make me happy, so
I gorged myself on all its fare. But oh,
the disappointment! the despair! the rage
I felt! I sought this hunger to assuage,
while yet I fed on empty promises
and nothing more. How very vain this is.

18 *Moreover, I came to hate all the works that I had labored under the sun to complete, works that, I came to see, I would only*

AND when in my despair I looked upon
the things I'd built, the works that I had done,
I came to hate them too. The pleasure they
had given me did not endure, to say

leave for someone else to enjoy after me.

19 And who knows whether he will be a wise man or a fool? Either way, he will take charge over all the works that I, in the pursuit of meaning, have brought to completion under the sun. I tell you, this just doesn't make any sense! It's meaningless!

20 And so I fell into despair' over all the works that I had done under the sun.

21 Let me review: When you have a man who has labored with much wisdom to accomplish as much as he can and to profit by it, and then he leaves his work to another, who has not labored with him in it, this just doesn't make sense and is like chasing the wind. 22For what is left for that man

the least. And when I realized that I must leave them all behind me when I die for someone else's pleasure, it was more than I could take. What was this striving for, for heaven's sake? FOR who knows whether he into whose hands these treasures fall will be a wise man or a fool? For pleasure will he waste and squander what I've done, or still preserve and care for them? My God, I thought, I've worked so hard! And shall it be for naught, or will there anything remain to show that I was here, to let the future know that here a wise man ruled, if only for a time? Is this too much to ask, O Lord? And so I cursed my progeny, and cursed my works as well. I tell you, nothing's worse than realizing at the end of life that all your labor, all that pain and strife, amounts to nothing more than vanity. How can this be? O God, how can this be?

AND so I sank into despair. My soul could find no rest, no peace. In all the whole long list of my accomplishments, not one appeared that gave my life beneath the sun the slightest bit of lasting meaning. Old and bitter, how I shuddered at the cold and clammy prospect of a nameless grave.

I had to make some sense of this, to save my sanity, at least. So this is my conclusion: When you have a man who, by his work and wisdom, profits greatly in this life, then dies, his fortune comes within the power of one who has not labored right there with him all that time. Who knows? He might just squander everything. It's hard to see why that should be. WE'D like to think that he *from all his work and striving with which he has labored under the sun?*

23 *For all his days he works and strives over many hard and diffi-cult matters; he knows many sleepless nights as well. This doesn't make sense either.*
24 However, if work is your life, that is, if you expect your work to make you happy and to give meaning to your life, if you think this is the way to know wisdom, then[s] *in this life there is nothing better for you than to eat and drink and to tell yourself that this is as good as it gets.[t] Even this,* this bit of con-solation, *is a gift from God, so I have seen.*

25 *For who can really enjoy life at all, who can make any real sense out of life or find any lasting meaning without God?[u]*
26 *For God gives wisdom, under-standing, and joy to the person who lives as he intends. But the sinner,* the person who scorns God and chooses not to live before him, *gathers much and collects many things, but in the end,* God will turn the fruit of that person's labors over to the one who serves God. I came to see this, and it seemed to me not to make any sense. *It was*

who earned this wealth might realize some boon
beyond the grave, but who can tell? Too soon
we all will come unto that fate, so why
this strife and struggle, if we cannot buy
with it some lasting meaning, or some peace?
WHY suffer all those sleepless nights? At least
we might enjoy some rest for our weary bones
if we didn't have to fret over what we own
and what we'd like to. Yet we do it just
the same. Does this make sense? I think we must
be mad or stupid. **WE** expect our work
to make us happy, and it really irks
us when we can't find meaning in it, or
it doesn't let us make enough to gorge
ourselves on everything our eyes can see.
If you think this is wisdom, son, then be
my guest and keep on saying to yourself,
"I'm having fun, I'm having fun," or else
you'll lose your mind. But please consider this:[u]
The wealth you gain, the peace and happiness
you know within this life, no matter how
enormous or how slight, befalls you now
because of God's good pleasure, nothing more.
FOR I will tell you here and now, before
you think me cynical, that none will find
contentment, purpose, joy or peace of mind
of any lasting sort apart from him.
FOR God provides these things, not on a whim
as some might think, but to the one who lives
his life to please him. Yes, to him God gives
these blessings freely. On the other hand,
the one who thinks that he can understand
his life apart from God, who chooses not
to follow him and serve him as he ought,
may prosper and grow rich, but in the end
he dies, like all of us, and he will spend
eternity in unquenched anguish while
the one who pleases God will know the smile
of his good pleasure and become the heir

meaningless, merely chasing the wind.

of that man's fortune. And I know you'll swear
that makes no sense, and so I thought as well.
But it is true; believe these words I tell.

ETERNITY IN OUR HEARTS

ECCLESIASTES

III

*Solomon shows that we are driven to discover
meaning and purpose in life because,
in fact, it is there, but only when we see life from
God's perspective
and according to his eternal plan.
Otherwise life makes no more sense for people
than if they were mere beasts.*

1 There is an appointed time for everything, and every matter[a] has its place under the heavens:[b]

PERMIT me to explain more fully what I've come to understand: Our lives will not make sense apart from God; but if we learn to see as he intends, we can discern the meaning of each matter in its place in his economy.[c] There is a space for every opposite beneath the throne of heaven; every mystery has its own

2 A time for giving birth, and a time for dying; a time for planting, and a time for uprooting what has been planted.
3 There is a time for killing, and a time for healing; a time for breaking things down, and a time for building.

and proper place. **THERE** is a time to bring new life into existence, and to sing the dirges of the dead; a time to sow good seed and, when it's had a chance to grow, to gather up the harvest. **THOUGH** to kill someone may seem repugnant to you, still, at times it's necessary, while we will prefer to heal at other times. To build can have its place as much as to destroy.

4 Weeping has its place, as does laughter; so also mourning and dancing for joy.

TEARS flowing down our cheeks and laughter, joy and merriment all have their place. We'll mourn the loss of loved ones, so we must not scorn

5 At times we must discard stones, at other times we gather them together; in the same way, there is a time for embracing, a time to refrain from embracing.

to dance for joy with them as well. **WE** throw large stones out of our fields so seed can grow, but gather them to build the barns to store our harvests. There's a time for love, I'm sure you will agree, but there is time as well to keep from love's embraces (I can tell you that, my friend!). **THERE** is a time to go

6 There is a time for seeking for things, and a time for letting lost things go;[d] a time for keeping and a time for throwing things away.

and look for something lost, but we must know when we have searched enough, and be content with losing things at times. At times we're meant

7 Sometimes we must tear things up, at other times we will need to sew them together; there is a time for silence and a time for speaking.

8 There is a time for loving just as there is a time for hating; yes, even a time for war, as also for peace.

to keep things, but at other times we'll throw them out. **WE** tear things up at times, you know? At other times we will repair them. Words and conversations have their place, absurd as they can be at times; which only goes to show that sometimes keeping quiet shows the wiser path. **THERE** is a time to love, but there's a proper time for hatred of some things as well; there is a time for war, and there is time for peace before the bar of heaven's wise counsel. Everything, you see, makes sense when seen in God's economy, although it may be difficult for us to understand at times. So we must trust that God knows what he's doing, even though we may not understand.

9 We asked, "What profit is there for laborers in all their work?"ᵉ

               WE asked, "And so what benefit do we derive from all our work in this short life, from what befalls us in our days beneath the sun?" **THAT** life

10 Well, I have come to understand the things that God has given as burdens to the children of humankind.ᶠ

11 God, you see, has made everything just right in its time and place; and he has, as it were, put eternity in the hearts of human beings, but not so that a person might find out or fully and completely understand what God is doing in all these things.ⁱ

can be an awful burden, filled with strife and sorrow, I will not deny. But can you see that God imparts to every man the burdens he must bear? **I** said before that all of these are gifts from God.ᵍ What's more, he has a single purpose in them all: for he has made us, every one, the small and great alike, with hearts designed to seek and know him. Hear me out, for what I speak you know is true, my son.ʰ Deny it not: we have the spark of deity and ought to live in consciousness of God each day. We'll understand things better if we stay within the scope of his eternal plan; however, we will never understand our lives as well as he, and so we must resolve to live by faith, that is, to trust his Word and follow in the path that he

12 So there really is nothing bet-   has given each of us, **CONTENT** that we

ter for us to do than to rejoice and do good throughout our lives.
13 For every person who eats and drinks and finds good in all his works has found the gift of God.

*14 For I know that whatever God does lasts forever; nothing can be added to it, and nothing can be taken away from it. It is per-*fect, as God intended, *God does all that he does, moreover, so that people might fear* [k] *him.* [l]
15 Yes, what has been is what will be, for God seeks pattern and consistency in all his works. [m]
16 And yes, under the sun, that is, as people pursue their lives apart from God, *wickedness is found where justice should be, evil where we should expect to find righteousness.*
17 But as I said to myself, God will judge both the righteous person and the wicked person; for there is a time and a place even for these in his economy. [q]

18 I saw that [r] God was allow-ing *things to come to persons as they did in order to test them, to show them that* apart from him *they are but beasts.*
19 For from the secular per-spective *humans and beasts are no different; their fates are the same.*

should take delight in simple, daily things
and do what good we can with what he brings
our way. **FOR** even simple things and deeds
of seeming insignificance can be
of everlasting value when the Lord
himself is doing them in us, absurd
as it may seem.[j] **AND** no one can improve
upon his works; for through them he would move
us to inquire of him, to fear and love
him, and to serve him all this journey of
our mortal flesh. **IT'S** true, as I have said,
that there is nothing new among the dead
or living; God has made it thus, and he
sustains it so as well.[n] Just so, might we
consider by what rationality
the world subsists, and wonder what might be
the explanation of it all?[o] **TO** see
life only from the secular point of view
will show us how chaotic, how askew
things are. Where justice ought to be, instead
we find all kinds of evil, as I've said
before, and wickedness in place of right.[p]
BUT when you keep the heavenly throne in
    sight,
you'll find contentment knowing God will bring
to judgment each injustice. Everything
that seems remiss he will redress; for he
intends that everything that is should be
according to his will and for his great
and everlasting glory in this state
in which we live. **THE** things that come our way
in life are sent from God, as if to say,
"Take this, and profit from it, but do not
omit to honor me, as creatures ought,
lest, failing this, you show yourself to be
no better than a beast." **FOR** can you see
that from a secular perspective man
and beast are just the same? What profit, then,
or what advantage comes to being men

They both die, being creatures of breath; there is no advantage to being a human being over being a beast.[s] *It's meaningless, I tell you, it's all meaningless.*[t]

20 Human beings and beasts all go to the same place—back to the dust from which they came.[u] *21 Who can know whether the spirit of a person ascends to a higher life or that of a beast merely descends to the grave?*

22 So from this point of view, I have seen that there is nothing better for a man than to try to be happy in the things that come his way in life, for this is his lot under the sun. For who will enable him to see what will come after him? No one, not when you look at life like this.[x]

if we're no different or no better than
dumb animals? The grave awaits each one
of us when this sad, brutish life is done,
and after that there's nothing. Why the fuss,
then? It's enough to make a good man cuss
and swear! Why struggle to make sense of things?
If all we are is beasts, and everything
is meaningless, why do we seek to find
some purpose and some lasting peace of mind?
IF in the end the dust awaits both man
and beast alike, since we're no different than
the animals; **AND** since there is no way
to know if there's a higher life someday
for us beyond the grave, why rack our brains
to make our lives amount to more than pain
and sorrow, like the other beasts?[v] Why not
accept our lot and live life as we ought
to, if we're only animals and not
the image-bearers of the Lord? **BESOT**
yourself with life's vain fare, my friend,
if this is all there is, if in the end
a gaping grave is all there is to greet
and gather you! Go on, my son, and eat
until you're full, and fornicate at will,
cavort, carouse and carry on until
you die, and leave off trying to make sense
of this your beastly plight! The vain pretense
of meaning is a hoax.[w] You might as well
consult your dog concerning heaven and hell
as any other fellow beast, although
they may insist they understand, they know
the truth. If life is nothing more than this,
this vain charade beneath the sun, desist,
my son, from wanting more than each day's vain
and fleeting fare, and learn to live with pain.[y]

NO ONE TO COMFORT THEM

IV

His gaze now fixed back on matters under the sun,
Solomon contemplates the injustice and
oppression that he has witnessed around him.[a]

1 Then I turned again to consider all the oppressions that have been done under the sun, and see there? The weeping of the oppressed,[b] and there is no one to comfort them. And their oppressors possess power, but there is no one to comfort them.

NOW as I turn my mind to think again on all the oppression that is done by men to fellow humans, this I see: the tears of the oppressed confront me, all their fears and sorrows, all their bitter sadness and their broken spirits. Who is there to stand with them? to comfort them and care for all their needs? Who weeps because they stumble, fall and perish? No one—not a soul. The mass of humans are too busy with their crass and selfish undertakings to give thought to the oppressed. Meanwhile, the ones who ought to care for them—their rulers—are too much concerned with aggrandizing power and such delights as with it come to feel the pain of those who are oppressed. What would they gain

2 So I commended those who are already dead more than those who are still alive.
3 Even better than both of them is the one who has not yet been born, who has not seen the evil things that are done under the sun.

by wasting time on them? **S O** given this appalling situation, I will bless the dead more than the living, since their woes are over. **EVEN** more, I bless all those who as of yet have not been born, for they are spared this awful vision of the way ungodly persons treat each other. Glad are they if never born; they've never had to see how cruel people can be, how great a fool one is to fill one's life with hate and jealousy and greed—as I have done at times throughout the years.

4 I have seen every work and every profitable thing that has

       I know, my son, you find the work that people do to have

been done, that it is the result of
the envy of a person toward his
neighbor; this too is vanity and
chasing the wind.

redeeming value. So do they. They salve
their guilty consciences with work from dawn
to dusk. Oh yes, I've seen them, working on
and on, no time for friends or family,
and driven by some foolish need to be
a little richer than their neighbor. Here
is more oppression yet: people hold dear
material things above all else—for so
we teach them to—so much that they forgo
all meaningful relationships, all art
and beauty, everything that's not a part
of making money, to devote more time
to this idolatry. We take the prime
examples of our precious youth and fill
their minds and hearts with mere material swill
and then expect them to behave like saints.[c]
And when they don't, we wail our loud complaint
against the generation we have made
the way they are. Oh what a dark charade

5 The fool folds his hands and
consumes his flesh.
6 One hand full of rest is better
than two hands full of labor and
chasing the wind.
7 Then I considered again vanity
under the sun:

we play! **PERHAPS** you'll say it's better then
to simply set all work aside. **THEN** men
could take it easy, slow the pace of life,
enjoy the simple things, and leave off strife
and chasing after a little more. **BUT** I
can see you know that this is just a lie
and feeding on the wind. Work has its place,
this much is sure; but if it's just to chase
vain riches, what's the point? But who can give
us any other reason now to live

8 A certain man was all alone;[d]
he had neither son nor brother,
and yet there was no end of all his
labor. And he was never satisfied,[e]
wanting everything he saw. "And
for whom am I working so hard
and depriving my soul of every
good thing?"[f] This too is vanity
and a grievous matter.

than to work to grow in wealth—and die? **I** knew
a man who lived all by himself. Now you
would think, with no one to provide for but
himself, no heirs or brothers, that he ought
to take it easy, work enough to pay
the bills, relax, enjoy his life. No way!
Like everybody else he could not get
enough of things. So he would never let
himself be satisfied and starved his soul
to feed his lusts. Each day he dug his hole

a little deeper, never stopping to
consider what a fool he was. Would you
call this man wise?

9 *Two are better than one, because*
they can share the fruit of their
labors together.[g]

       IT seems to me that two
who work and share their lives together do
much better than one all alone. For thus
we learn to care for others and to trust
and love, though this does not come easily.
BUT it is worth the effort, you'll agree;
for two will complement each other. They
have different wants and needs, and each one may
see life a little differently. If one
should falter, then the other one will run
to his assistance. It is hard if you
should fall and be alone, with no one to
come to your aid, no one to care. **AND** there's
a certain joy from having one who cares
for you, who lies beside you in your bed
each night and keeps you warm and fills your head
with thoughts of love. I pity those who this
companionship and intimacy, this bliss,
have never known. **WHO** stands with them
   against
their enemies? While two can make defense
when an assailant comes, one all alone
will not prevail. If he had only known
a true companion and a friend to aid
him, he might not have fallen.[k] But he made
himself sufficient, boasting he could make
it on his own, and he would undertake
to carve his path in life without the need
of anybody else to share his greed
or wealth—a self-authenticating man,
I guess you'd say. And what is sadder than
the self-authenticated man alone
with all his wealth, and never having known
to love, or care, or give? I tell you, when
we teach our children that life's greatest end

10 *For if one falls,*[h] *his companion*
can lift him up. But woe to the
person who falls and is alone,
with no one to help him up.

11 *Also, if two lie down together,*
they will be warm; but how can
the person who is alone stay
warm?[i]

12 *And while they may over-*
power a man alone, two can
stand against an attacker; and a
cord composed of three strands is
not easily broken.[j]

is wealth and all that it can buy, we mess
their minds and blight their souls, yes, we oppress
them, making them conform to our own view
of life and robbing them of what is true.

13 A poor but wise young man is better than an old and foolish king who is no longer willing to be enlightened.[1]

AN old and foolish king who will not learn
to do what's right and true is in his turn
just as oppressive as a tyrant. He
will rule to satisfy his lusts: Trust me,
I know. I'd rather have a wise young man
to rule than one who does not understand
and will not learn the law of God. **ALTHOUGH**

14 For he is taken away from prison to go forth as ruler, even though he was born poor in his kingdom.

he comes from prison—Joseph did, you know—
or from the poor, just like my father, he,
if he will live beneath the heavens, will be
a better king by far. Ah, how I long
for former days, when I was young and strong
in wisdom, not in worldly ways, when all
the rulers of the earth came here to call
upon my wisdom. That was long ago,

15 I have seen those who are living and going about under the sun[m] *with the second young man who stands after the first one.*
16 There is no end to all the people, to all those living before him; and those who come after him will not be happy with him,[n] *for this too is vanity and striving after the wind.*

however; things have changed. **AND** yet, al-
    though
that wise young man rules well, the people will
abandon him. **FOR** they will search until
they find a ruler who will promise to
fulfill their every lust. You see, they do
not really want a wise man for their king,
but someone who will give them everything
their foolish hearts desire. And though they ought
to thirst and hunger to be wise, they're caught
by their own lusts, and they will choose a man
to rule them who pretends to understand
their needs and longings, whether they are wise
or foolish. Meanwhile, he has set his eyes
on gaining power, so he will tell them what
they want to hear, and though they really ought
to seek a wise man, they will make this fool
their king instead. I know, for when my rule
was known for wisdom, wisdom could not stand

when wealth and mirth and power on every hand
began to be the order of the day.
So I forsook my wisdom for the way
of foolishness, and now I am an old
and foolish king. But let it not be told
of me—please God!—that when I reached my end
I was content with feeding on the wind.°

HONEST
TO GOD

ECCLESIASTES

V

Solomon warns against duplicity before God,
among rulers, and with oneself and others,
and counsels contentment
with one's work as the most that people
can hope for under the sun.

1 Guard your feet whenever you go to the house of God; and draw near to listen rather than offer the sacrifice of fools, for they do not know that they are doing evil.[c]

HOW brazen and dishonest people are with their religion.[a] They will go as far with it as suits their needs;[b] so they attend the services and sing the hymns, and when they have to, give a little money to the Lord. But do they live as one should do who's made a vow to God? Don't kid yourself. Among their friends their faith is on the shelf. They go to service not to hear the Word of God, but so that they can tell the Lord what he should do for them.[d] They think that he exists to make them happy. He should be ecstatic just to see them! They are fools who think such evil pleases him who rules the worlds.

2 Do not be too quick to speak or to offer a word in the presence of God, not even in your heart. For God is eternal, and you are of the earth, so let your words be few.

REMEMBER, God knows every-thing.
He knows our hearts when we before him bring our worship, and you can't fool him. So take a good look at yourself before you make your next appearance before the Lord. And go to listen, not to speak, for he will know just what you need. **WHY,** any fool can spout a lovely prayer or sing a hymn about his faith. His words are mindless, like a dream, although to people looking on they seem impressive. Not to God.[f]

3 For the dream comes by much effort, and the voice of the fool with many words.[e]

4 Whenever you make a vow to

DON'T make a vow

God, do not be tardy in fulfilling it; for God has *no delight in fools.*[g] *Fulfill your vows.*

you don't intend to keep. Make sure somehow you do what you have promised. It's the fool who takes a vow because he thinks it's cool or just another pious duty he should do, but never really plans to see it through. God is not pleased with this.

5 *It would be better not to vow at all than to vow and not fulfill it.* 6 *Do not allow your mouth to cause your body to sin, and do not try to tell God's messenger that your vow was a mistake.*[h]

IT would be better not to vow at all, than should you fail to keep your word with God. **DON'T** let your foolish mouth betray you so you get in trouble, having lied to God. Don't try to say your vow was a mistake. You should have thought about that first, my son. You could have just declined. But oh, you looked so good before your friends there when you said you would perform a vow—a real religious guy! So now you risk the wrath of God. Just try to talk your way around his anger. He will frustrate everything you try to be or do until you're honest with him and begin to love him and to understand what he requires of you.

7 *For in many dreams is foolishness, as also in many words; instead, fear God.*

FOR words are cheap, just like the dreams you have while you're asleep. God wants your heart, my son, not just a show. Get right with him before you to him go.

8 *If you see oppression of the poor and abuse of justice and righteousness in the country, don't be surprised at the matter; one official watches over another, and there are others over them.*[k]

WHY should it shock you when you see the poor oppressed, when men abuse the law, ignore true justice and hate righteousness?[i] What can a man expect when all throughout the land are people playing games with God?[j] Oh, they're accountable, for sure, but everywhere you look the higher-ups avert their eyes and take the bribe as well. Does this surprise you? Well, it shouldn't. **WHAT** the people need are governors who care, who really heed

9 *But the land will profit through all this if the king is out in the*

fields working for himself.[l]

what people say, who come among them where they work and listen to them as they share their fears and burdens. But the king prefers his palace and his chalice and his furs. The problems of the people never reach his ears; he's far above their plaintive speech.

10 *The one who loves money*[m] *will not be satisfied with money; and whoever loves wealth will never have enough. This too is vanity.*

SO what do people do who have to live in such a situation? Well, they give themselves to the pursuit of wealth, as we have seen. But those who do will never be content with money, or with any kind of wealth. If they are honest they will find that this is vanity and chasing wind.[n]

11 *When good things abound, they also abound who consume them;*[o] *so what do the owners of wealth get out of this, except to watch their wealth disappear?* 12 *The working person's sleep is pleasant, whether he has a little or a lot to eat;*[q] *but the abundance of the rich person does not allow him to sleep well.*

FOR when their wealth increases, then begin their troubles. They will spend as much (or more!) as they can earn. Their wealth goes out the door as fast as they can bring it in.[p] They buy more than they need and hardly even try to keep their spending down. **AN** honest man who works an honest day upon the land will be content with what he has. He'll sleep in perfect peace each night. But riches keep the wealthy man awake. He frets about his debts, how his investments will turn out, and if he'll have enough so he can get a little more. What vanity! I'll bet you know some people just like this. **AND** here's

13 *I have seen a terrible evil under the sun: riches being kept by their owner to his hurt.*[r]

an even grosser evil: when, in fear he'll lose it all, he simply buries all his wealth or hides it in some secret vault away from everybody's eyes. What good to him—or anyone—is that?[s] He could at least indulge himself a bit; but then his neighbors all would know, and soon all men would try to steal his riches. **MAYBE** he could hide them in some foreign treasury, or in some realty deal or other scam. Some crooked guy will take his wealth and scram

14 *Then those riches perished through some wicked deal, and he had a son, who now had no one to support him.*

15As he came forth from the womb naked, so he will return as he came. He will take nothing in his hand of the fruit of all his labors.

16 And this is a terrible evil: As a person is born, so shall he die, and what profit will he have who has labored after the wind?

17 All his days he eats in darkness,[t] with great vexation, sickness and anger.

18 So here's what I have seen: It is good and beautiful to eat, drink and see good from all one's work done under the sun during the few days of the life God gives, for this is one's lot.[u]

19 Also, every person to whom God gives riches and wealth, God has enabled him to eat of these and to receive his lot and to rejoice in his work. This is a gift of God.

20 But he will not often remember the days of his life, for God occupies him with the gladness of his heart.[v]

before he knows it, and he's left without a cent to feed his kids. They'll turn him out into the street, AND he will go to meet his Maker naked. What a way to greet the God whom you have spurned for all your days! BUT this is how it is in many ways: We enter life with nothing and we leave it just the same. And in between we grieve because we can't make sense of life. SO all our work and all our fretting, all the small stuff and the big, is meaningless. Our life beneath the sun is vanity and strife.

SO what's to do? Here's my advice: Go learn contentment. Take what life will let you earn, enjoy it all you can and don't complain. Perhaps you'll come to see that all your gain in life is just a gift from God that he allots to you so you'll begin to see that he exists and that he cares for you. AND if he gives you wealth, enjoy that too. Rejoice in God's good gifts, but let them lead you to consider him, to see your need for him and understand his wondrous grace. Then seek him; don't let wealth somehow erase all your awareness of his being and his love. CONSIDER him, and take your stand with those who live beneath the heavens, or your wealth will just distract you more and more.

FULL LIVES,
EMPTY SOULS

VI

Solomon once again takes up his argument
that life is more than things.
People can fill their lives with every
imaginable good thing
and still be miserable, if they fail to satisfy
the deep longings of their souls.

1 There is an evil that I have seen under the sun, and you see it everywhere:[a]
2 a person to whom God gives riches, wealth and glory, so that his soul lacks nothing of all that he might desire, and yet God does not allow him to eat from it, because a foreigner consumes it. This is vanity and a very great evil.

NOW here's another evil I have seen: people live godless lives and try to wean themselves away from God. It happens all the time: **GOD** lets a man acquire no small amount of riches, wealth and honor, such that he should have enough to give him much abiding happiness, as much as he could ever want. And yet the Deity does not allow him to enjoy his wealth;[b] instead some stranger comes by guile and stealth and takes it from him. Granted, this is wrong; but if that man had made his soul as strong as his portfolio, he would survive this tragedy, still glad he was alive.[c] The godless man, however, cannot see why such a gross injustice ought to be, at least, not done to him.

3 If a man fathers a hundred children and lives many years, even though they be many years, but his soul is not satisfied with the good things he has, and if he does not have a decent burial, I say a miscarriage is better off than he is.

THE same is true for those who father many children too. If they cannot be happy with the good that God has given them, as all men should, but spend their days pursuing wealth instead of with their families, when they are dead their children, just as eager to conserve their wealth, will not provide what they deserve, a decent burial, but scrimping all the way, will dump them in the ground and call it even.[d] Why, a child untimely born is better off. **IT** never sees the morn

4 For it comes in futility and goes

in darkness, never having seen the light of day, *and its name is covered in darkness.*
5 *Also, it never sees the sun, and is more at peace than that man.*[e]
6 *Even if he lives a thousand years twice, but is not able to appreciate*[g] *the good* in his life, well, *do not both end up in the same place?*

and never knows the vanity of life beneath the sun. **IT** never knows the strife of those who fret and worry as they try to make their lives make sense before they die.[f]

THE man who won't appreciate the good that God has given him, although he should, and should desire to know this One who's blessed him so—which is for all of us the best that we can do in life—this man is just as good as dead. Until we learn to trust and follow God, our futile lives will be unsatisfying; we will hopelessly careen from one thing to the next until we end up buried on some lonely hill or underneath some tree. If this is all there is to life on this terrestrial ball and all its vain diversions; if the end of our existence is the grave, well then, it's all a waste of time, won't you agree?

7 *You see, a person like this, all his work goes to satisfy his fleshly needs,*[h] *and yet his soul is never satisfied.*

8 *So what difference does it make whether one is a wise person or a fool?*[i] *What is there for the poor man who knows how to live his life*[j] *before the living?*
9 *To each of them, under the sun, what the eyes see is better to them than what benefits the soul.*[k] *This also is vanity and chasing after the wind.*

FOR everybody knows there's got to be much more to life than just this flesh and bones. But when a man devotes himself through groans and strivings just to meet his fleshly needs and never listens to his soul or heeds those deeper longings, **THEN** it matters not if he's a wise man or a fool. And what about the poor and humble man? He knows how he should live his life, and yet he goes around like everybody else, content with discontentment, sulking, driven, **BENT** like everybody else on getting all he can from life. And though his soul might call to him from time to time, he doesn't hear. He's far too busy with his cheerless, drear pursuit of happiness to listen to his deeper longings. And I think that you can see the vanity in this.

10 We've seen all this before,[1] and it is well known what human- kind is; and they are not able to dispute that which is stronger than they.[m]

BUT we have seen this all before. We know that we are more than flesh, that somehow we connect with God. And yet we act like we expect no more from life but more and more of life.[n] But all our days we know the constant strife that comes from living like a beast while in our heart of hearts we know that, being men, we're different somehow. **SO** we seek to find some satisfaction for our troubled minds

11 For people make many attempts to explain their vani- ties,[o] but how does this help them?[p]

in vain philosophy, but there's no end of foolish efforts to declare again what life is all about; and none of them completely satisfies us, for they hem and haw their clumsy way through every vain attempt to clarify, define, explain and justify our lives, but all to no

12 For who can know, under the sun, what is good for a person during the days of his vain life- time? He will live them like a shadow. For who, under the sun, will be able to tell a person what comes after him?

effect. **FOR** none of them can truly show us what is good, or true, or beautiful. In place of what is true they give us dull and changing guidelines; where we seek the good they tell us that our circumstances should suffice to guide us; where we ask that they might show us something beautiful, they say it's only in your eye. And so, apart from God, it goes: We suffocate our hearts— our souls—and live like shadows, foolish men devoid of substance,[q] tied to earth, and then we die. And who of our philosophers can tell us what beyond the grave occurs?

GOING TO
EXTREMES

ECCLESIASTES

VII

By presenting a series of opposites,
Solomon tears open the veil revealing the heart of
wisdom and exposing the foolishness
of trying to make sense of life apart from God.[a]

1 A good name is better than good ointment;[b] and the day of one's death is better than the day of one's birth.[c]

2 It is better to go to a house of mourning than to a house of feasting, for this is the end of all people, and the living takes it to heart.

3 Sadness is better than laughter, for the one who has a sad face may have a happy heart.

4 The heart of the wise person is in the house of mourning, but the heart of the fool is in the house of revelry.

5 It is better to hear the rebuke of a wise person than for a person to

I know this much, my son: good ointment's nice
but having a good name's better, even twice
as good. The day you die is better than
the day you're born, for at the end a man
has something he will be remembered by,
while at his birth he's nothing more than high
parental hopes. It's what he does between
these times that matters—that's what I have seen.
DO you desire relationships that last?
Then stick by people in their need; stand fast
with others, even in deep loss.[d] A fool
will be their friend when all is well. How cruel
to seek their blessings and refuse to be
a blessing to them in their time of need.
BEWARE the man who's always making jokes
and laughing at a hat's drop or the stroke
of every hour. His heart is only set
on foolishness and mirth. You'll never get
a man like this to share your sorrows. Learn
to feel the pain of others, and discern
their grief. You'll find that this will fill your heart
with happiness, when you know to impart
a sympathetic gesture. SO the wise
man is the one who learns to care, who tries
to be there for his friends when they're in pain.
The fool can only think in terms of gain
for him; he's always out for fun.

JUST so,
you're always better off, my son, although

listen to the song of fools.

*6 For like the sound of thorns
under a pot, such is the laughter
of fools; this too is vanity.
7 For oppression makes a wise
person sad, and a gift corrupts the
heart.
8 The end of a matter is better
than its beginning; patience of
spirit is better than arrogance.*

sometimes it hurts, to heed a wise man's stern
rebuke. Take his advice, for you will learn
much more from him than from the song of fools,
though they be many. **FOR** the fun that rules
their hearts is fleeting, like the thorns you light
to start a fire beneath your pot each night.
THE wise man weeps to see oppression's dart;
and every bribe contaminates the heart.
THE way a thing works out is better than
the way it starts, for then it's just a plan,
a hope, a prospect. Get to work and bring
it to a sound conclusion; then they'll sing
your praises. But be careful not to let
your heart get proud. Just wait, my son, you'll get
the praise that you deserve.

*9 Do not be hasty in your spirit to
be angry, for anger rests in the
bosom of fools.
10 Do not ask, "Why were the old
days better than these?" For wisdom does not lead you to ask this.*

        BE careful not
to let your heart get angry, for you ought
to keep in mind that it's the fool who lets
his temper rule his life. **AND** just forget
about "the good old days"—as if they were
as great as that. The wise man will prefer
to look ahead and try to make the most
of what's before him, not to mourn the ghost
of times that never were.[e] **YOU** might receive

*11 Wisdom together with an
inheritance is a good thing and
will profit those who see the sun.*

a nice inheritance, but don't deceive
yourself, for without wisdom, wealth is just
another path to foolish living.[f] Trust

*12 For wisdom is a shelter just as
money is, but the advantage of
the knowledge of wisdom[g] is that
it preserves those who have it.*

me, son, I know. **I'VE** come to see that there
is much to gain from wisdom. It will care
for you like riches, more, in fact, because
it never fades away. For wisdom was
what God intended for us, more than wealth;
and they will know prosperity and health

*13 Look at the work of God, for
who is able to straighten that
which he has made crooked?*

who learn to live as God intended, **FOR**
it's vain to think that any person or
that any thing could change what God intends.[h]

14 Rejoice when good things hap-

WHICH brings me to contentment once again:

pen to you; and when evil things come, look, God has made the one as well as the other, so that people will not be able to find out anything that comes after them.[i]

God gives us all our lot in life. He brings us good at times, at other times he stings us with adversity. But here's the point: We shouldn't let ourselves get out of joint when trouble comes, or when we find it hard to make sense out of things. Just trust the Lord, my son. He always does what's good and right; He's with us always, whether day or night.

15 I've seen it all in the days of my vain living: There is a righteous person who perishes in his righteousness and a wicked person who lives a long life of evil.

I tell you, son, I've seen it all throughout my years of foolishness. I've learned about the way of wisdom by a foolish route and seen some things I could not figure out. Like this: A man who lives a righteous life, who never fails his friends or causes strife but always does what's right and true, is nailed onto a cross by wicked men who've failed the test of righteousness. Meanwhile, a man who lives his life as wickedly as he can lives long and prospers. WE might want to say to that,[k] Don't try to live the wise man's way

16 [j]Don't be too righteous, and don't be excessively wise; why should you kill yourself trying?

or strive for righteousness. It doesn't pay, for people just get angry, and they say, "So who's he think *he* is?" Who wants to die before his time has come? Not you; not I.

17 Don't be too wicked, and don't be a fool; why should you die before your time?
18 It's a good idea to take a bit of one thing and, at the same time, not to let the other go out of your hand.

I think instead I'd say, it's better not to go to the extreme of evil. WHAT you ought to do is set your sights to be a wise and righteous person and to flee from evil, though you'll never get away from it completely. Though you cannot stay your hand from wickedness entirely, you can reach for wisdom with the other.[l] Do

19 Wisdom strengthens a wise person more than ten rulers living in a city.
20 However,[m] there is not a righteous person on the earth who always does what is good and

this, and you'll find that WISDOM gives more strength
than powerful rulers, though they go great lengths to guard their city. FOR to think that you can free yourself from sin and always do the wise and righteous thing is to deceive

never sins.

21 *Also, don't take to heart every word that you hear spoken; you might hear your servant cursing you.*

22 *For you know, you have your-self many times cursed others and not really meant it.*

23 *I tried all this by wisdom; I said, "I am going to be wise," but it escaped me.*

24 *What I sought was far from me and extremely mysterious. Who can acquire it?*

25 *I set my heart to search out wisdom and an explanation of things, and to know the evil and foolishness of folly.*

26 *And I discovered more bitter than death is a woman whose heart is full of snares and nets, whose hands are chains; before God, he is better who escapes her than the sinner who falls into her hand.*

27 *"Look, I have discovered this," says the Worship Leader, adding everything up to find an explana-tion for it all,*

28 *which my soul is still seeking but has not found, "I have found one man in a thousand,*[p] *but I have not found a wise woman in all these."*

yourself."[n] Accept your sinfulness,[o] believe
that God is good and brings you good in all
your days, and set your course to heed the call
of wisdom. **AND** another thing: Don't be
thin-skinned, you know? Don't take it personally
when you hear someone say an unkind thing
about you. Fight the urge to want to zing
them back in kind. **YOU** know that you have said
a thing or two you didn't mean. Instead
just bear it all with grace. **I'VE** thought a lot
about these things. In fact I said, "I ought
to be a wiser person, so I will."
How foolish. Wisdom's ways escaped me still.
I'D drifted very far from where I first
began, and lived so foolishly, rehearsed
such evil in my time, that wisdom seemed
beyond my reach, like something I had dreamed
about but never could expect to gain.
I set my heart to know and to explain
the foolishness that was the life I'd known,
to see if I had learned, or if I'd grown
at all. **AND** here's what I have found: The grave
is better than a woman who enslaves
you by her wiles and leads you to rebel
against the ways of God. I have to tell
you, you are better off in God's eyes to
resist than to surrender to her. Do
yourself a favor: Be content to find
a woman who won't fill your silly mind
with dreams of power and promises of love.
SO here's my meaning: Now that push to shove
has come in my own fleeting life, **I'VE** found
the way of wisdom, though in part. It's sound,
but few will ever know it. They prefer
to satisfy their flesh and will defer
the search for wisdom to some later time
in life—say, after they have reached their prime
and sowed their share of foolish oats. Like me,
they will surround themselves with vanity

and think they're really living now. Until
they wake up one day with a void to fill
deep in their souls, and not a thousand more
of this world's vain conceits could heal that sore.
I added woman after woman, since
I thought that this was living (how I wince
to even mention it). But it was all
in vain. Deep down inside I hungered for
much more than merely sex or power, much more
than all the foolish things I'd known. What I
was seeking was to know before I die

29 But consider what I have what life was all about. **AND** this is it:
found: God made men upright, God made all people so that they would fit
but they have sought out many into his wise and righteous plan. But we,
explanations of their own. supposing we knew better than did he,
set out on our own way in life. Instead
of finding what we sought, we end up dead
and wonder what went wrong. But who can tell
us, as we pass beyond the grave to hell?

CIVIC WISDOM

ECCLESIASTES
VIII

*Solomon offers advice on the ways of people
in civil society—before kings,
in matters of justice and injustice,
and in the works of wickedness and righteousness.*

1 Who is like the wise man, and
who knows the interpretation of a
matter? One's wisdom enlightens
one's face; it transforms even a
harsh countenance.[a]

SO who is like the wise man—who can know
the meaning of it all, and who can show
us what this vain and foolish life is all
about? For wisdom, though it seems a small
and unimportant thing compared to power
or wealth or having fun, is what this hour
most urgently requires. True wisdom can
transform the most debased and wretched man
and make his face shine like the sun.[b]

2 I say, Guard[c] *the king's word,*
because of your oath which you
made before God.[d]

3 Do not go hastily from before
him, and do not take your stand
in an evil matter against him,
for he will do whatever he pleases.

4 Because the word of the king
has authority, who will say to
him, "What are you doing?"[f]

5 The one who keeps his com-
mand will not experience evil;
and the heart of a wise person
knows time and justice.

SO hear
a little wisdom, son, and hold it dear:
Be careful to obey your king. Before
the Lord, you must obey his every word
and honor him. **DON'T** walk away and turn
your back on him; don't be too quick to spurn
your lawful rulers or to join against
them in conspiracy. Think: what defense
will save you when your evil is exposed?
The king will crush before him all of those
who think that they can overthrow him.[e] **FOR**
his word has all authority; therefore
who is so foolish as to think that he
can stand against him, or that royalty
would even deign to answer when he tries
to get an explanation? **DON'T** despise
the king's command, but keep it, and you'll find
that evil will not haunt your heart and mind
or ruin your life.[g] Oh, there may come a time
to stand against the king; but all that I'm

6 For there is a just time for every delight, when the evil that weighs on a person is great upon him.

7 For no one knows what will come to pass, for who can declare what will be?

8 No one has the authority to restrain the wind with the wind,[h] and no one has authority over the day of death; and no one may be discharged during war, and evil will not deliver those who practice it.

9 All this I have seen, and I set my heart to every work that has been done under the sun, in which a man has ruled over another to his hurt.

10 Therefore I have seen the wicked buried,[j] when they go in and out of the holy place, and they are forgotten in the city in which they did this.[k] This also is vanity.

11 Because the decree against an evil deed is not executed quickly, the heart[l] of the children of humankind is filled within them to do evil.

determined you should understand is that it takes a wise man, one who's focused at eternal truths, to know when justice calls one to resist the king. **WHEN** evil falls like bricks upon you, therefore, know, my friend, that every joy you seek its proper end and time possesses. Justice may not let you know it at this time, but do not get discouraged. **WHO** can tell you what will come to pass or what will be? For no one from the future is available to you.
And this is just to say again: Don't do what you may live to rue. Be patient. **YOU** can't rule the wind, or give a schedule to the day that you will die; and if we were at war what are the odds you'd be deferred?[i] Just so, you cannot hope to beat the odds of doing evil. For remember, God's the One who waits to punish every act of disobedience. **THESE** are just the facts, my son. I've seen it all, what life is like apart from God, where selfish people strike at one another, lie and cheat and steal, oppress, deceive and take advantage. Real attractive, don't you think?

　　　　　　　　　　　AND then they die. The funeral's nice enough: we give the guy his due; his loved ones weep; his friends all say they'll miss him; then we bury him away from sight, and everyone forgets him. Well, you just can't mourn forever, can you? Tell you what, this is as futile as it gets.
OR maybe not. Another thing upsets me: when an act of wickedness, condemned by all, is subject to appeals, and hemmed and hawed about by lawyers endlessly, young people, who are fools at heart, will see that justice is a joke and evil can be profitable.

12 Although a sinful person does a hundred evil things and lives a long life, yet I know that it will be well with him to fear God before his face.

BUT though a wicked man
lives long and gets away with evil all
his life, yet in the end I know he'll fall
before the justice of the Lord. The man
who fears Almighty God, who takes his stand
in life beneath the heavens, will be blessed.
To fear the Lord is more than good: it's best.

13 But good shall not result to the evil person; and will he not lengthen his days like a shadow, he who does not fear before the face of God?[m]

BUT evil men, as I have said, will find,
though life is long and wickedness is kind
to them while they're alive, that God has no
compassion for the unrepentant. Though
their lives are long, they're like a shadow. When
they stand before the sovereign God such men
will perish, and without a trace.

14 There is a vain thing that is done upon the earth, that there are righteous persons to whom things happen as though they were wicked, and there are wicked persons to whom things happen as though they were righteous. I say, This too is vanity. 15 So I commended pleasure, for there is nothing better for a human being under the sun except to eat, drink and be merry, for this shall remain with him in his vexation all the days of his life that God gives him under the sun.

AND so
it puzzles me to think of how things go
in life, when righteous folks, who live to please
the Lord, are made to know the pains of these
exasperating days, while wicked ones
are wealthy, happy and content. My son,
I say that this is vanity. **SO** this
would seem to be the formula for bliss:
Just live it up here while you can; enjoy
as much of life as you can grab; employ
your wits to serve your lusts, and let the rest
fend for themselves. Is this the very best
that you can do with all the blessings you
have known in life from him, the only true
unchanging God? Well know that if you live
without regard for him, then you will give
yourself to foolishness like this, and hope
that all your vanities will help you cope
with your unanswered questions and your doubts.

16 When I gave my heart to know wisdom and to see the things that had been done on the earth, though I had never slept by

AND this is why I tried to figure out
the way of wisdom, and to see this life
and all its folly, all its people rife
with fears and tears, from God's perspective. **I**

day or night,"
17 then I saw every work of God,
that a person is not able to figure
out what has been done under the
sun. Whatever one might seek to
know, one is not able to discover
it; and although the wise person
should say, "I know," he is not able
to find it out either.

have seen this much: No matter how we try
to make sense of our lives, to find some peace
and joy in all our working to increase
our happiness, though we might never sleep,
the challenges we face are just too deep
to fathom on our own. Oh, some pretend
to have the answers without God. They end
up dead and in the grave and having to
explain themselves before the Lord—as you
will have to do one day. So don't deceive
yourself and think that somehow you'll achieve
some understanding of it all apart
from God. Such thoughts come from a foolish
     heart.

ALIVE
(AT LEAST)

Solomon warns of the inevitability of death
and counsels contentment with the gifts of God
in the face of life's fading glories.[a]

1 *For I have taken all this to heart, and I have concluded that the righteous person, the wise person and their servants[b] are in the hand of God;[c] whether love or hatred shall befall, one does not know; anything can happen.*

2 *It's the same for everyone; for the righteous and the sinner, the end result is the same. For the good person and the clean person, as well as the unclean person, the one who offers sacrifice and one who does not, as it goes with the good person, so with the sinner; the one who swears and the one who is afraid to swear.*
3 *There is an evil in all that is done under the sun, that there is one result for all; and the heart of the children of humankind is full of evil; madness is in their hearts throughout their lives, and afterward they die.*
4 *For anyone who is chosen[f] to*

SO here's the upshot of it all: each one of us, without regard for what we've done in life, or whom we know, or what place we might occupy in our society— each one is in the hand of God,[d] and he decides for each of us just what will be for us throughout our lives, if we will know the warmth of love, or if we will be so despised that life will be a constant pain and aggravation. We can't hope to gain the slightest insight into what will be ahead for us; we'll have to wait and see. **THAT'S** right, it's just the same for everyone: The righteous person and the one who's done his share of wickedness, the person who is quite religious and all who eschew such practices, the one who swears a blue streak[e] and the one who is afraid to use his tongue for wickedness. The simple fact is this: when life is done and we have packed it in, the grave awaits us all. **SO** here's the greatest evil that this earthly sphere presents: that everyone alike will die. Our hearts are filled with evil, don't deny it; yes, and madness too. We give our lives to vanity; each one's a fool who strives to make himself a name, but what a shame, for after all the years of work, the game is over and the grave's the victor. **YET** we press ahead with all our strife and bet

*stay among the living, there is
hope, for as they say, a live dog is
better than a dead lion.*

*5 For the living know that they
are going to die, but the dead don't
know anything. They no longer
have a reward, for the memory of
them is forgotten.*

*6 Their love, their hate and their
zeal have already perished; they
will have no portion forever of all
that is done under the sun.*

*7 So go on, eat your daily bread
with joy, and drink wine to your
heart's content; for God has
already approved your works.*

*8 Let your clothes be white all the
time, and don't forget to put oil on
your head.
9 Live your life to the full with the
woman you love all the days of
your vain existence that God has
given to you under the sun, all
your vain and empty days; for
this is all you have to show from
all your labors that you have
worked at under the sun.
10 Everything your hand finds to
do, do it with all your strength, for
there is no working or discovery*

on life, that somehow it will all make sense
to us. But this is just a vain defense
of ego. We amuse ourselves and say,[g]
    "A live dog beats a lion dead." OK,
it's true, the living still have hope. **AT** least
they know they're going to die and be a feast
for worms;[h] the dead know nothing. No reward
awaits them either, when their sad and hard
existence finally ends. The memory
of them is swept away, just as the sea
erodes a beach. **THEIR** loves, their hates, their
    zeal
all perish with them. Death at last will steal
whatever portion they have garnered through
their years of striving, when they come into
their final disappointment in this life
beneath the sun.

            AND yet, although it's rife
with disappointment, make the most of it
while you're alive. Drink up, enjoy your bit
of foolishness beneath the sun.[i] As I
have said, God gives you every blessing; try
to find contentment while you can.

                LOOK sharp,
smell nice,[j] impress your colleagues, take the warp
and woof of life in stride. **AND** give your love
completely to the darling woman of
your dreams. These are the gifts of God to you;
this is the best that anyone can do
beneath the sun. Why gripe and moan your life
away, pursuing vanity and strife
at every turn? Relax. Appreciate
God's gifts. For life is short; the grave awaits
us all. **WHATEVER** comes your way, apply
yourself with diligence, my son, and try
to make the most of it. For once you're dead,
that's it. There's nothing more that can be said

or knowledge or wisdom in Sheol, which is where you are going.

11 I considered again, and I saw under the sun that the race does not go to the swift, nor the battle to the mighty; bread does not come to the wise, nor riches to the discerning, nor favor to persons of knowledge; but time and chance overtake them all.

12 Moreover, one does not know when one's time is coming. Like fish caught in an evil net and birds in a snare, so the children of humankind are snared when an evil time falls upon them suddenly.

13 I also came to see this as wisdom under the sun, and it seemed great to me:
14 There was a small city with a few people in it, and a great king came against it, surrounded it and built great siege works against it.
15 And there was found in it a poor but wise man, and he could

or done or learned in hell, which is where you
and everybody who refuses to
submit to God on high are bound.

FORGIVE

me if I seem to judge the way you live,
but life is very short, and when you choose
to live apart from God, my son, you lose.
Stop trying to make sense of it without
consulting him. I know you're filled with doubt;
well, so am I. How else can one respond
when everything that should make sense has gone
completely opposite of what it should?
The swift don't win their races, and the good
don't strike it rich; the strong fall to the weak;
the wise go hungry; and the ones who seek
advantage in great learning fail. For time
and chance catch up to everybody.[k] I'm
no different, nor are you. **AND** worst of all
is this: we cannot know when death will call
on us. Why, it could be today, who knows?
And when disaster comes, and when it shows
its ugly face all unexpectedly,
we're like a fish that's hooked beneath the sea,
or like a bird that's caught fast in a snare:
There's no way out. Time's up. No matter where
you turn or how you try to twist your way
out of his grasp, he's going to have his day.

HERE'S one example more of wisdom blown
by those who try to make it on their own
without the Lord, and it is typical
of how folks think beneath the sun: **A** small
and sparsely populated city was
attacked by a much greater king. He caused
great siege works to be built against it and
prepared to breach its walls. **BUT** then a man
was found within the city, just a poor
and humble man, but he had wisdom for

have[l] *delivered the city by his wisdom, yet no one paid attention to that poor man.*

16 As I said, *"Wisdom is better than strength." But that poor man's wisdom was despised, and no one listened to his words.* 17 *The words of wise persons heard in quiet reflection are better than the shouts of a ruler in the midst of fools.*

18 *Wisdom is better than all the spears you might muster, but one sinner destroys much good.*

the rulers as to how to save their town. His plan just might have worked, for it was sound, but no one took him seriously because he wasn't from nobility but was a peasant. "What do peasants know about such things?" And so they threw the fellow out. **THOUGH** wisdom is superior to strength— a point that I have tried to make at length already—yet the rulers scorned the man and laughed at his suggestions and his plan. **THEY** tried to rally their poor people by vain promises that they would fight and die together and would gain the victory— the talk of fools. Today they might be free if they had listened thoughtfully unto that wise but humble man. **NO** weapons you can muster will prevail against the sound advice of wisdom, which is only found beneath the heavens; on the other hand, one sinner who resolves to take his stand beneath the sun and follow policies and plans devised without the Deity's advice, although he does the best he can, will bring destruction to his native land.[m]

THE BLESSINGS OF COMMON SENSE

ECCLESIASTES

X

*Solomon compares the knowledge
gained by common sense with his assertions
about life under the sun,
suggesting that the way of wisdom
and of seeking God is far to be preferred
to the way of the fool, apart from God.*[a]

I know that what I'm saying is for you
confusing, difficult and even new,
but it's just common sense. If you could see
as I have come to see it, you would be
convinced that what I've learned from all of my
experience is true, and you would pry
yourself away from every worldly view
and give yourself to finding God anew.
It's simple, really; but the problem is
a man is naturally inclined to his
own foolish views, which seem to him to be
more valid than the ways of God, which he
ignores.[b]

1 Dead flies make a perfumer's oil stink, and a little foolishness weighs heavier than wisdom or honor.[d]

AND so, just as dead flies can make
a rich perfume abhorrent, those who take
their own opinions over God's are doomed
to ruin.[c] **YOU** see, the wise man's heart
is groomed

2 The heart of the wise person tends to the right, but the heart of the fool to the left.[e]

to follow what is good and pure and true;
the fool, however, only wants to do
what makes him happy for the moment. **SO**
he goes about his business, like some know-
it-all; but having nothing in his soul

3 And even when fools are going about their business, they lack depth,[f] and they say to all that they are fools.

to guide him, he careens out of control
in front of everyone. **DO** you contend
that you are right in something? Then defend
your views! Yes, even if someone in power

4 If the ruler's spirit flares up against you, do not abandon your position; for soundness puts great sin to rest.

gets angry, starts to threaten and to glower
at you, don't walk away and just deny
what you're convinced is right. Be firm, and try

5 I have seen an evil thing under the sun, like a foolish ordinance from a king's mouth:

6 foolishness in high places, while worthy[h] persons abide in low places.

7 I have seen servants riding on horses and princes going about like servants on the earth.

8 Whoever sets a trap for someone else will fall into it;[i] and a serpent will bite whoever makes a breach in a wall.

9 Those who quarry stones get hurt by them, and the person who cuts down trees can be injured by them.
10 If the ax is dull and a man does not sharpen its edge, he has to work harder; but he profits who has wisdom.[k]
11 If the serpent bites without being charmed, there is no benefit to being a charmer.
12 A wise person's words bring favor; but the lips of a fool destroy him;

to put your case convincingly.[g] You know
that what I'm telling you is true. AND though
some king or ruler promulgates a law,
if it is foolish, don't be overawed
by him, but work to set it right. I tell
you, this is a condition made in hell
when people are indifferent to bad laws
or when they hesitate to act because
they fear a foolish ruler. THERE are lots
of fools on thrones, exuding royal rot
while able men, good men, are kept from power
when they might save a nation in its hour
of need. I would your store of common sense
provoke to get you to revolt against
your foolishness and turn to God. You know
it makes no sense when common servants go
on horseback while their noble masters walk.
YOU know that those who scheme, or plot,
    or stalk
the innocent can in their foolishness
be caught; and what a horrifying mess
a man falls in who tries to break his way
through someone's hedge and finds a snake to pay.
YOU know that certain kinds of work can be
a little risky—cutting stones or trees,
for instance—so you take precautions, right?[j]
It's common sense: YOUR ax has lost its bite,
so would you rather work a little more
or sharpen up your blade? As I before
have said, a little wisdom saves much pain.
OR would you pay to see a man who claimed
to be a serpent charmer, if his snake
attacked him as he was about to make
his pitch? WELL, just the same you know it's
    true:
A wise man's words bring favor to those who
receive them, but a man who does not know
the Lord, and only has his wits to go
on, is a menace to society.

13 *he begins talking foolishness, and in the end it is evil madness.*
14 Yet *the fool continues to spout off.*[m] No *one knows what will happen; and who can tell what will next come to pass?*
15 A *fool's work wears him out; he doesn't have enough sense to call it a day.*[n]
16 Woe *to you,* O *land whose king is a youth and whose princes feast in the morning.*[o]

FROM first to last his words can only be
an exercise in vanity. **AND** yet
he rambles on—I know that you have met
a man or two like this. He talks like he
has seen the future, knows just what will be
and most of all, what you should do about
it. **ON** and on he goes like this, throughout
the day, until he finally drops. At last
he stops, but then the chance for wisdom's past,
and only foolishness remains. **O** land
that suffers underneath the foolish hand
of young and selfish rulers, rulers who
know just exactly what they need to do
to line their pockets and secure their base
of power—O what a sad and awful waste!—
I say, You are a most unhappy land.

17 Blessed *are you,* O *land whose king is of noble birth and whose princes eat when they should, so that they can become strong and not merely drunken.*

BUT O how happy, on the other hand,
the kingdom that is governed by both wise
and selfless rulers, who can hear the cries
and feel the pain of all the people and
who give themselves to try to understand
how they can serve their nation best. Alas,
such rulers seem a blessing of the past.

18 Neglected *buildings become run down, and a lazy man's roof will leak.*

SO use your common sense, my son. You know
neglected buildings fall apart. Just so
your hungry soul.[q] You know a roof will leak
above a lazy man; and need I speak
to you of how elusive wisdom can
be for the careless and indifferent man?

19 People *eat for merriment, and wine makes* their *lives happy; and money is the answer for everything.*[p]

WE seek for happiness and hope to find
all that we need in things: We've lost our mind
if we expect that food and drink alone
will bring us happiness or will atone
for our iniquities before the Lord
on high. We act like wealth's the final word
in life, but what a joke.[r]

20 So *do not revile the king* when you are in *your bedroom, and do not curse a rich person* when you are in *your inner room; for a*

WE fear the king
so much we wouldn't utter anything
against him, even in the privacy
of home and bedroom, for we know that he

little bird will carry the sound of your words, and a winged creature will make the thing known.

will find us out. We cater to the rich
and wouldn't slander them—though we may itch
to sometimes—for we fear offending those
who strut around in all the latest clothes
and fashion, since we hold out hope that they
might toss a little excess cash our way;
we lock our lips and dare not criticize—
no wonder there is such a dearth of wise
men in our midst. It's common sense, my friend.
Your foolishness will kill you in the end.

MAKE THE MOST
OF IT—
WHILE YOU CAN

*Given that life is short
and young people
are not inclined to think about eternity,
Solomon advises
making the most of it while you can.[a]*

1 Send your bread upon the waters, for after many days you will find it again.[b]

2 Divide a portion to seven and even to eight,[c] for you do not know what evil may come upon the earth.[d]

3 If the clouds are full, they pour heavy rain on the earth; but[e] whether a tree falls to the south or to the north, from the place where it falls, there it will lie.

4 He who is careful[f] about the wind will not sow; and the one who watches the clouds will not reap.

5 Just as you do not know which way the wind will blow,[g] or how bones are formed in the womb, just so you do not know the works of God, who makes everything.

YOU have to take your chances, make the most
of every day, before you're just a ghost
and all the bills come due. So take a chance
with what you have; get on the floor and dance
a little, make a few investments, try
new things, don't be afraid that you might die
before you take the time to live. **INVEST**
yourself in many things. You'll find it best
if you diversify; uncertainty's
the only certainty in life, so please
expand your interests, friends and holdings.
   LEARN
to make sound judgments based on fact; discern
the possibilities before you act,
but keep in mind this one essential fact:
each one of us has limits: Any tree
might fall this way or that, but it will be
where it was planted when it dies; don't try
to be what you cannot. You fly too high
and you may find the sun too hot.[h] **BUT** don't
be timid; being overcautious won't
do you or anybody any good.[i]
Just work as hard as anybody should
who has the gifts and opportunities
you have. **FOR** life takes faith or, if you please,
"informed unknowing."[j] You will never know
with certainty the way the wind may blow
or how a child develops in the womb.
You can't know everything; there must be room

6 Sow your seed in the morning, and do not slack your hand in the evening, for you do not know whether one or the other will succeed, or whether both of them will be good.

7 Light is sweet, and it is good for the eyes to see the sun.[k]

8 If a person should live many years, let him rejoice through them all; but let him remember the days of darkness, for they are many. Everything that is coming is vanity.[l]

9 Be glad, young man, during the days of your childhood, and let your heart be filled with good during the days of your youth; and let your heart and whatever you see lead you. But know this, that for all these things God will bring you to judgment.

10 So clear the scales from your eyes![m] *Put away wickedness from your body—because childhood and youth are nothing but vanity!*[n]

for faith. But there is One who knows it all, and that is God, who made it. You won't fall by having faith in him. **SO** give your best in life; work hard, and don't forget to test the waters that the Lord will bring your way. And try your hand at many things. Don't say "I can't do that" when you have never tried. You never know what good may take your side until you test the waters and apply yourself in many different ways. That's why they say, "Sow in the morning and at night; you just can't tell which one of them is right for you, or maybe both will work." **AH,** life is good, my son; with all its woes and strife, it's still the only game in town. As long as you can see the sun, then put a song upon your lips and make the most of life! **AND** if it pleases God that you survive for many years, then go rejoicing on your way before your earthly days are gone, which soon enough will be. And then the dark eternal nothingness sets in, the stark reality that life is more than time and things and fun and spending all the prime years of your life in the pursuit of vain ideas and empty hopes. **BE** happy, plain and simple, while you're young and life is full of things to see and do.[o] And don't be dull at heart; relax, rejoice and let your heart's desires and all your wildest dreams impart direction for your soul. But keep in mind that one day every one of us will find ourselves before the judgment seat, and then we'll learn our life's true worth and value, when Almighty God declares his view of how we've spent our vain and fleeting days.[p] **SO** now, wake up! Clear out your brain! And put away all foolish notions that in any way keep you from seeing life the way God meant

for you to see it. Youthful years get spent
too quickly, and the prime of life is done
before you know it. Don't be foolish, son,
and think that you can grasp the meaning and
the deepest things of life, or understand
what wisdom is, or peace, or lasting love
and joy apart from knowing God above.

THE WHOLE
OF A PERSON

ECCLESIASTES

XII

Solomon brings his argument to a conclusion,
calling upon his readers to consider their Creator
and devote themselves entirely to him.

1 Remember[a] your Creator in the days of your youth, before the evil days come, and the years arrive in which you say, "I have no delight in them";

2 before the sun becomes dark and the light and the moon and the stars become dark;

3 when those who guard your house tremble, and the strong men are bowed; when the grinders fail and are few, and those who look out the windows become dark;

4 and the doors that go out to street are shut, and the sound of the grinding mill is lowered, and one rises at the sound of a bird and all the daughters of song are brought low.

5 Also people are afraid of a high place and of terrors on the road; the almond is despised,[e] the locust

THUS my advice, my wayward-leaning son,
is that you give your youth before it's gone
to knowing God. For otherwise you'll find
in days to come you'll have no peace of mind,
and nothing that provides you so much fun
and entertainment now beneath the sun
will matter in the slightest. AND this view
of life you're oh so desperately clinging to,
your search for meaning in possessions, power
and wealth, will lose its luster in that hour
WHEN by the trembling in your
   wrinkled hands,
the stooping in your back and shoulders[b] and
your brittle, broken teeth and failing eyes,
you come reluctantly to realize
you're getting old[c] and death is near, and all
your foolish hopes have vanished, and the pall
of nothingness is settling down upon
your wasted frame. Your carefree days are gone,
AND your desire to go out on the town
has shriveled, and your appetite is down—
which doesn't matter, since digestion is
at any rate a chore[d]—and in the midst
of night you waken at the slightest sound—
a little bird that's singing on the ground
beneath your window—yet while you're awake
you find it harder every day to make
out what is being said around you. AND
irrational fears beset you: you won't stand
up on a high place any more, or go

becomes a burden, and all desire is lost.[f] *For one* must *go to one's eternal home, while mourners go about in the street.*

6 Remember your Creator *before the silver cord is a thing of the past and the golden bowl is crushed,* before *the spring jar is broken and the wheel to the well is crushed.*

7 *Then the dust will return to the earth which gave it, and the spirit will return to God who gave it.*

out for a walk or take a stroll because you're sure that thugs and muggers will assault and rob you, maybe even kill you on the road. Exotic foods that mean so much to you today will all have been forgotten—broken teeth and almonds do not mix that well, as I am certain you agree. And walking, well, it makes you tired to even think about.[h] See, time's expired for you, my son, when all of this begins to settle in, and then you'll know death wins at last. **YOU'LL** look for comfort in your *haute couture.* You'll think your precious treasures ought to brighten things a bit—your silver chains and golden bowls[i]—or maybe what remains there in the well of all your great ideas.[j] But none of if will satisfy or please you any longer, if it ever did. **AND** then you'll have to face the thing you hid from your consideration all those years: It's dust-to-dust time, friend, and all your tears and pleadings won't do any good. Your flesh is headed for the ground, where it will mesh with worms; your spirit, in the meantime, wings its way to God, who gave it and who brings it to his judgment seat when life is done. Just see if he'll accept your life of fun and games as worthy of his holiness forevermore.[k] Oh no, my son, the mess you're making of your life today will be your ruination for eternity.

8 As the Worship Leader I[g] say, "*Vanity of vanities; all of it is vanity!*"
9 *Now, in addition to being a wise man, the Worship Leader taught knowledge to the people, and he investigated, searched out*

MUST I remind you, son, of what you know already, that as far as wisdom goes this Worship Leader has no peer?[l] **THAT** I was looked upon by all and sought out by great kings from near and far, who listened to my words and went back to their lands to do what they were taught by me?[n] That I searched out

and arranged many proverbs.
10 The Worship Leader sought to
acquire things^m that bring plea-
sure, and to write righteous words
of truth.

11 The words of a wise person are
like goads, and those who master
them are like well-driven nails;
they are given by one Shepherd.^p

12 But beyond this, my son, be
warned: There is no end to the
making of many books, and
much study wears you out.

13 When all has been heard, this

and wrote three thousand proverbs?^o Do you doubt
my wisdom, knowing what you know? I tried
to have it all, the things that fueled my pride
and satisfied my lusts, along with truth.
But this was just a vain conceit of youth;
for lust, when fed, cannot be sated but
will cry for more, and happily you put
up with its cravings, while the righteous words
you thought were so important fly like birds
and are forgotten. BUT as you can see
from my experience, if you want to be
as sharp as goads and have your words command
respect from others, if you want to stand
like firm-fixed nails, as solid as a stone,
then seek for wisdom. Do not take your own
ideas or wishes as of consequence;
the only certain hope and sure defense
against eternal disillusionment
is wisdom, gained from knowing God. Present
yourself before that caring Shepherd now
before the grave consumes you and you bow
before his wrath. Do not suppose that you
will find what you are seeking if you go
to every worldly sage or every book
that's ever written. You can look and look
among those dreary tomes to find some sure
and lasting meaning, something sound, secure
and satisfying. But you'll only wear
away your brain. You won't find anywhere
but in the Lord the meaning that you seek.^s
SO hear me out, my son, and I will speak
this one last thing: You want to know the way
to have a full and happy life. I say
to you that life is only in the Lord.
You're searching everywhere to find some word
of truth to set your mind at ease. What you
are looking for is God. You're hoping to
discover life in all its wonder and
its joy and satisfaction. UNDERSTAND

is the end of the matter: Fear[d] *God, and keep his command-ments, for this is the whole of what it means to be a man.*[r] *14 For God will bring everything to judgment, everything that is hidden, whether it is good or evil.*

what I am saying: When you know and fear the Lord you find that life, and not just here and now, but for eternity. **AND** he is patient. He will wait, believe you me, for you to seek him out. So do. Begin at once to get to know the Lord. For in the end, his judgment seat awaits us all, and only those who fear him will not fall.

ENVOI

I

JOHN 14:6

*Jesus said to him, "I am the way,
and the truth, and the life; no one
comes to the Father but by me."*

Then Jesus said to him, "You seek the way
to God, that you might break out of the fray
of all this strife beneath the sun and know
how you can really live; well, I can show
you, for I am that way. You seek the truth,
that you might come to know what from your
　　youth
has to this day eluded you. Well, I
am what you seek. You wish to find a high
and happy road to walk, to know a life
of meaning, joy and victory over strife.
I tell you, friend, I am the life you seek.
Believe me when these words to you I speak."

MATTHEW 11:28-30

*Jesus said, "Come unto me, all
who are weary and burdened
down, and I will give you rest.
Take my yoke upon you, and
learn from me, for I am humble
and meek of heart, and you shall
find refreshment for your souls.
For my yoke is easy, and my burden is light."*

"So come to me, all you whom life has beat
down, worn down and exhausted; come and meet
the One who can provide your rest. Come pull
with me within my yoke, and learn the full
and happy truth that I can teach you. For
I am a humble man, and even more,
I am your Savior who is meek of heart;
and you shall find refreshment for your part
with me. So come and see: The yoke I hold
out to you is not hard to wear, though old
or young you be; and take up with me now
my easy burden. I can show you how."

STUDY GUIDE

Introduction

You are about to begin the study of Ecclesiastes, one of the most difficult and misunderstood books of the Bible. At the same time, it is quite relevant for our materialistic, relativistic, sensualistic, pragmatic and uncertain times. This study will give you an opportunity to discover more about yourself and the times in which you live, and how these relate to the reality of the eternal God and his purposes.

Think About This

1. One of the themes that Solomon (the author of Ecclesiastes) will pursue in this brief essay is the difference between the secular life—which he refers to by the phrase "under the sun"—and the life of knowing and loving God—life "under the heavens." These two approaches to life are very much evident in our own day. What differences between them can you identify?

2. Solomon will also insist that people cannot find any lasting meaning in life apart from committing themselves to God. Yet people are always seeking some meaning or purpose for their lives. What are some ways that secular people try to make sense out of their lives and discover something truly lasting and meaningful?

3. Do you see any evidence that these various ways of making sense out of life are not bringing the satisfaction people seek? Should this make it easier or harder for them to come to know the one true God? Why?

4. Solomon will affirm that everything in life is good as long as we see it from God's point of view and use it with grateful hearts in obedience to him. This includes our relationships, the work we do, our civil governments, all the beautiful things in life and much more. Is it really possible that these things might have something to do with a person's relationship to God? Explain.

5. Given these themes, what would you like to see happen in your own life as a result of your study of Ecclesiastes? What goals will you set for this project?

STUDY 1

This is life as Solomon saw it from an earth-bound point of view,
and this is life as modern philosophers see it.
And they are not alone. Countless numbers of ordinary men and women
look at life this way, too.

STUART OLYOTT

Read Ecclesiastes 1

Many have written about the apparent loss of meaning and direction that people—particularly young people—are experiencing today. Television, popular music and film are filled with images of people desperately seeking to discover what life is all about. Try though they may, many are having a hard time making sense out of their lives. You may sometimes feel that life is little more than chasing the wind, just as Solomon did.

Think About This

1. We seem to have an inbuilt drive to make sense out of our lives, to be able to understand why we're here, what we're supposed to be doing and what life is all about. We seek answers to these kinds of questions from a wide variety of avenues. What roles do things like family, friends, education, work, popular culture and leisure activities play in people's struggle to make sense out of their lives?

2. Do you detect a sense of "chasing the wind" in our world today among the people you know? That is, do you see people who are frustrated, worried and uncertain concerning what their lives are all about? People who are struggling to distraction, if not despair, to figure out the big questions of life? In what ways do you see this?

3. How do people you know try to deal with the uncertainty and the lack of meaning and purpose they find in their lives, as well as the fears and doubts these bring with them?

4. In general, would you say that ours is a society that tries to make sense out of its existence "under the sun" or "under the heavens"? What makes you think that? Do you think that is a good thing? Why or why not? Is there any sense in which we need a little more of one of these? Explain.

5. From what we have seen thus far, are there any aspects of Solomon's story with which you can particularly identify? Which ones?

> *He means to expose what we nowadays call the secular view of life:*
> *a life without any absolutes, a life without the certainties*
> *of the revelation of God's Word, a life lived out of values*
> *generated by man without reference to God,*
> *a life that expects lasting satisfaction from earthbound things.*
> *Qoheleth wants to show how such a life has to be meaningless*
> *and must end in disillusionment in time, not to mention eternity.*
> *To heighten the drama of his argument,*
> *he gives vivid presentation of this position as if it is all there is!*

GORDON J. KEDDIE

> *So what is the use then? What do men achieve for all their sweat, worry,*
> *and stress? What then is life? Is it merely the dreary rhythm*
> *of ceaseless activity? What is left for man for all his trouble?*
> *There must be a better answer somewhere else.*

WALTER KAISER

STUDY 2

Because secular man cannot reckon with his sin and rebellion
he finds that life must turn out to be a bitter disappointment.
When man has believed so supremely in man
and his life becomes intolerable because his goal of being his own god
has failed to accomplish the perfect life that he expected,
his response inevitably becomes one of nihilism and complete despair
of all his cherished values. His only option is totally to hate himself
and all of life; and his lone goal is to reduce all to disorder
in the vain hope that somehow a new order will emerge.

MICHAEL KELLEY

Read Ecclesiastes 2

Have you noticed how many angry people there are? We hear about hate crimes, road rage, hate groups and the "angry American." Music (especially certain rap music) is filled with angry lyrics, and television and film present many individuals who are either just about to or already have gone over the edge. What's everyone so angry about? Could it be that they have arrived where Solomon did—at the point of hating life and everything in it—and are simply seeking some way of venting their bottled-up rage?

Think About This

1. You are no doubt familiar with the mocking question, "Are we having fun yet?" Think about this question and ways that you have heard it used. What does the person who uses this question mean to imply? Can you see in this any of what Solomon was talking about in Ecclesiastes 2? Explain.

2. There seems to be a sense among people today that no one way of life will give us all of the satisfaction we deserve. We need to break a few rules, check out some new adventures or surround ourselves with more things. In what ways have you seen this in the areas of advertising, pop music and television? What does this suggest about happiness and purpose in life?

3. Solomon was seeking happiness and meaning in life. But what does that mean? How would you define these terms?

Happiness:

Meaning:

4. Between happiness and meaning, which is more important? Why? How can you tell when you are beginning to desire the lesser of the two above the one that is more important?

5. Think of a time when you really lost it, that is, when you just blew up over something. Was this in any way related to your perception that something or someone was thwarting your pursuit of happiness or your struggle to make sense out of your life? Talk about this situation with the others in your group. Do you think you may have been experiencing some of what Solomon described when he said that he "hated life"?

> *What is the point of it all? Where is lasting satisfaction to be found?*
> *It is not in a high level of education, with a string*
> *of letters after my name and a reputation for being learned.*
> *It is not in having my every material desire supplied.*
> *It is not in my arriving at the top rung of my particular ladder.*
> *Nor is there even a lasting sense of fulfillment in having*
> *worked hard all my life. None of these things, in the long run,*
> *turns out to be worth while. What is the life worth living?*
>
> STUART OLYOTT

> *The purpose of life cannot be found in any one of the good things*
> *found in the world. All the things that we call the "goods" of life—*
> *health, riches, possessions, position, sensual pleasures,*
> *honors, and prestige—slip through man's hands*
> *unless they are received as a gift from God and until God*
> *gives man the ability to enjoy them and obtain satisfaction from them.*
> *God gives that ability to those who begin*
> *by "fearing," that is, believing, Him.*
>
> WALTER KAISER

STUDY 3

Read Ecclesiastes 3

Deep inside we all have a sense that there is some meaning or purpose to our lives. We *matter*, we tell ourselves, and so does life itself. Evolutionary and postmodern philosophers may go on about the ultimate meaninglessness of existence, but they *act* more like their words and works have some larger purpose and significance. We go to school, make career choices, marry and raise a family, lay up for retirement and try to stay abreast of world events as best we can. Why? The cows in the field across from my home have no concern for such things. What drives humans to such transcendent experiences?

Think About This

1. People go through various stages in trying to make sense out of their lives. Even as children, in the games we played, the friends we made and the roles we assumed from time to time, we were trying to figure out something about who we are and why we're here. Think back on your own childhood. Can you recall your earliest experience of thinking about things such as meaning and purpose in life? What did that involve?

2. Solomon avers that everything in life has its place, everything makes a contribution to God's overarching plan to bring good to people. He means us to under-

stand that this includes the bad things as well as the good. Think back on a situation or event that happened to you that you considered to be really bad at the time but that, in retrospect, you can see brought good into your life. Summarize that situation and then share it with the other members of your group.

3. Solomon says that human beings have "eternity in their hearts," that is, that human beings were made in God's image so that they could know him. Think about what you know of world cultures. What cultural evidence from history can you point to that might support Solomon's claim?

4. Toward the end of this section, Solomon uses a form of argument known as *reductio ad absurdum,* reducing a premise to its absurd but logical conclusions. The premise is that "men are nothing more than animals." Where does Solomon take this argument? How does he try to show that believing such a premise is contrary to the way people actually live?

5. The idea that humans are just a higher form of animal is a widely held view. Why do you think so many people willingly accept the words of philosophers and teachers telling them this?

> "He has also set eternity in the hearts of men."
> This is the basis of the ache that men and women feel
> for something more enduring than this life.
>
> GORDON J. KEDDIE

> If we cannot alter the dispensations of God,
> let us set ourselves down to the more profitable work
> of altering our own judgment of them.
>
> CHARLES BRIDGES

STUDY 4

What we want, we define in terms of need, and since
it is inevitable that what we believe we need must be good,
our personal goals, thus qualified,
become the driving imperatives of life.
Ambition becomes necessity; necessity becomes a god.

GORDON J. KEDDIE

Read Ecclesiastes 4

Oppression takes many forms, but at bottom it is simply what we do without regard for the consequences to others in order to get what we want. In our day, while we give lip service to not harming others, we are encouraged from youth to get whatever we can in life by whatever means possible. Why does it shock us so when this leads to shameful behavior, corruption or violence?

Think About This

1. Solomon touches on the oppression he sees in the worlds of work, relationships and politics. Can you see any reflections of his concerns in our own day?

2. What is it in people that leads them to think that oppression—in any of its several forms—is a legitimate means to achieve their ends? Have you ever felt this way? Explain.

3. How does Solomon describe or allude to the state of those who are oppressed? How does oppression make them feel? What does this do to them?

4. Virtually everyone will agree that oppression is bad; yet many people practice it without calling it such. What are some other names by which oppression makes its presence known in our society?

5. Do those who oppress others—by whatever means—usually end up content and feeling good about themselves? Explain your answer. How might you help someone who was oppressing another person to see the wrong in it?

> *What is Qoheleth saying? That meaninglessness is inevitable*
> *in a life lived in terms of under-the-sun secularism.*
> *Oppression continues year after year, even human achievement*
> *owes more to envy than to altruism, and, in any case,*
> *wealth and power per se seem to exacerbate*
> *rather than ameliorate the emptiness that so many people feel.*

GORDON J. KEDDIE

> *Who can count how many over-ambitious executives*
> *have learned the truth of these words, without ever reading them here?*
> *And who among us does not know a score of wives*
> *who look back with longing to the days when their now*
> *successful husbands had less responsibilities,*
> *less anxieties and less money—but more time to enjoy*
> *what really matters most in this life?*

STUART OLYOTT

STUDY 5

*If we be not rich in God we shall never be truly rich in anything,
regardless of our material possessions. The good things of life
are only truly good by reason of the goodness of God's presence
that must accompany them.*

MICHAEL KELLEY

Read Ecclesiastes 5

There are undoubtedly many ways in which people practice dishonesty today. By playing at religion—going through the motions without really having their hearts in it—they are dishonest with God. By concealing their real motivations—in relationships, business and so forth—they are dishonest with one another. And by continuing to tell themselves that all this dishonesty is just the norm, they are dishonest with themselves. Is it any wonder that real, lasting happiness escapes so many people when their lives are filled with so much dishonesty?

Think About This

1. Can you think of a time when someone's dishonesty toward you caused you harm, embarrassment or disappointment? Explain.

2. We are forever hearing the complaint about hypocrisy on the part of religious people. That is, others perceive that people are not honest about their reasons for being involved with religious faith. Why do you suppose it is so easy for people to fall into being dishonest with God?

3. I remember a time I was caught being dishonest about a relatively small matter. I was humiliated, and rightly so. Can you think of a time when you were

exposed as being dishonest in some way? How did it make you feel about yourself? What came of this experience?

4. Money—or at least the pursuit of it—tends to breed dishonesty on a large scale. Why do you suppose this is so? Is there any way to protect ourselves against it?

5. Implicit in Solomon's argument in Ecclesiastes 5 is that if we're honest with God, we're likely to be honest with ourselves and others. Do you agree? Why or why not?

Unless God is in the picture, a person's predicament is hopeless.
But once he is seen as the Giver of every good thing in life,
the recipient will not only want to rejoice in his gifts,
but to worship and serve him.

STUART OLYOTT

Man must begin as a believer and worshiper
if he is ever to enjoy living as God intended him to live.

WALTER KAISER

STUDY 6

People never seem to learn from the experience
of previous generations, and continue to look on wealth
as the road to satisfaction. Their hopes are always disappointed.

STUART OLYOTT

Read Ecclesiastes 6

What is it about money and possessions that drives us to think this is what life is all about? We have seen no end of people who had it all only to end up miserable and full of regrets at the end of their days. Still we press on to get more and more of this world's goods in the vain belief that just a little bit more will bring the contentment we seek. We would do well to heed the advice of Solomon and spend more time cultivating our souls and less time filling our lives with trifles.

Think About This

1. What is the allure of money and possessions? Why do you suppose these hold such a strong attraction for people?

2. Certainly money and possessions are not evil. God gives these gifts to people to be enjoyed by them as expressions of his goodness. But the Bible tells us that *the love* of money is a root of all kinds of evil (1 Tim 6:10). Can you think of some examples of how the love of money—and all that it represents—has led to evil?

3. The apostle Paul would say that people who are devoted to money and possessions have made an idol of created things, serving these rather than the God who gives them (Rom 1:18-23). How would you define *idol*? What are some ways that money and possessions become idols for some people?

4. How might a person begin to know when he or she is paying too much attention to the things of this world and not enough to the needs of his or her soul?

5. What advice would you give for keeping money and things from becoming idols? That is, how can we learn to see these as God's gifts and use them in a way that will honor him and keep us from pursuing them as ends in themselves?

> *Death ends whatever meaning there might have been.*
> *Is this the basis on which you want to live out your days?*
> *Is this all that you can make of the world around you?*
> *Is this your response to the manifest evidence of God's existence,*
> *goodness, and claims upon your life?*

GORDON J. KEDDIE

> *God alone can satisfy the soul, whether a man possess much or little.*
> *Man must first recognize the poverty of his soul*
> *before he can hope to become rich in anything.*
> *Those who labor only for the mouth will not find satisfaction,*
> *but those who hunger and thirst after righteousness will be filled (Mt. 5:6).*

MICHAEL KELLEY

STUDY 7

*When Qoheleth speaks of the need of wisdom,
it is God's wisdom he has in mind. True wisdom is never divorced
from the words and work of God. Qoheleth is a theocentric
antiabstractionist. For him, wisdom does not derive from age,
intelligence, or experience in themselves,
but from the interaction of the directive, revealed truth of God
and the responsive human mind and heart.*

GORDON J. KEDDIE

Read Ecclesiastes 7

Often it is in the extremes of life that we discover truth, meaning and purpose. When sorrow and suffering assail, when we are filled with unmitigated joy and happiness, in the midst of conviction or vindication, great wealth or extreme poverty, success or disappointment, then we discover what our lives are really about. In Ecclesiastes 7 Solomon hopes to stretch thin the veil of experience so that we might be able to see into the heart of wisdom and consider how we might better know the will and ways of God.

Think About This

1. Can you think of a time when you were pushed to some extreme in life? What did you experience then? What did you learn from that experience? How did it help you to see more clearly what the meaning of life is about?

2. In many ways ours is a time of people going to extremes. We have seen extreme sports become a new fascination. Some people devote themselves to gaining extreme wealth, while others renounce the world and commit to lives of extreme poverty. Some have turned to extremes of violence, while others seek extreme peace through drugs or other forms of escape. What do you make of this? Why are people so eager to experience something extreme in their lives?

3. Certainly Solomon is not counseling us to seek extremes in order to discover meaning in life. At the same time, none of us can avoid the experience of these various extremes from time to time. How should we regard them, and what can we do to make sure they help us to discover life's real meaning and purpose?

4. If wisdom is to be found not *in* the extremes but merely *through* them, then we must look to some other source to help us sort out our experiences and gain what God wants us to gain from them. This is what it means to live "under the heavens" rather than "under the sun." What role can the Bible play in this? How can wisdom-seekers help one another to gain the benefit this revelation from God provides?

5. If we try always to live at the extremes—anger or indifference, depression or exhilaration, wealth or poverty, intellectual achievement or emotional fulfillment, comfort or risk, or any other extremes of life—we will miss the life of wisdom altogether. What advice would you give to someone who is seeking to make sense of his or her life by always pursuing one or another of life's extremes?

> *Man is constantly meddling with endless questions instead*
> *of the path of duty—the way of safety—the only way to God.*
>
> CHARLES BRIDGES

> *Wickedness in man's experience is no mere happenstance,*
> *no accident of nature, but a deliberately sought-after course*
> *of behavior. Man does not practice evil fortuitously;*
> *he acts from a mind-set that carefully calculates both its means*
> *as well as its ends. Sin in man is an active principle,*
> *ever seeking more territory to conquer.*
> *Far from having a tangential place in his experience,*
> *it is the controlling dynamic in all that he does.*
>
> MICHAEL KELLEY

STUDY 8

The king's commandment—when to keep—when to resist it—
the right manner of keeping or resisting—
this is sometimes a time and judgment calling for great discernment.
It is not man's natural prudence that sufficeth.
It is the wise man's heart—the heart enlightened
by the knowledge of God and his will—the heart possessed
by "the Spirit of wisdom"—here alone is the safe discernment.

CHARLES BRIDGES

Read Ecclesiastes 8

The decisions, policies and programs of civil governments can sometimes be maddening. Which of us has not felt like taking the law into our own hands at times, so great has been our disappointment or our anger at some decision or rule made by the government? But we need to remember that government, for all its occasional fallibility and foolishness, is a gift of God to provide for an orderly and good society.

Think About This

1. What ways can you see in which government serves the good of the people it governs?

2. Why is it reasonable to expect that governments will make decisions at times that strike us as foolhardy?

3. How should we respond to such actions? Are we expected to obey laws that we regard as foolish or wasteful, or that put us at some inconvenience? Can you think of some examples of laws like this?

4. There may come a time when we feel strongly in our conscience that we simply cannot obey some government decision or law. Examples of this may be a law that compels us to perform an action we consider immoral, or a law that curtails our freedom of religious expression. In a society of law, what is the proper recourse for the believer?

5. Psalm 72 and 1 Timothy 2:1-8 teach us to pray for our civil authorities. Take a look at those two passages. What are some ways that you can pray to help your government take more of an "under the heavens" approach to its duties?

*Abuse of authority is the rule in most of the modern world.
Even in nations blessed with the checks and balances
of a long tradition of personal freedom and the rule of law,
injustice is rife, and the oppressed wage constant battle
against those who simply want to lord it over others
and take advantage of them.*

GORDON J. KEDDIE

*To know the self-revealing God is to know that his will
is being done and that this must issue in
the blessings of God's people and the overthrow of injustice
and oppression and every other contradiction
of the mind and will of God.*

GORDON J. KEDDIE

STUDY 9

*This is the world—all that it can give. And yet to see men
of large and comprehensive minds—
living as if there was no God to whom they are accountable—
no heaven or hell to receive them for ever—
or as if these states were painted shadows, instead of Divine realities!
This surely is besotted blindness.*

CHARLES BRIDGES

Read Ecclesiastes 9

Every one of us is going to die. That's the hard reality of life. If life is nothing more than material self-indulgence, then we waste a lot of time with all our complaining, griping and worrying. We need to get at the real business of living it up while we can! But something inside us clamors for more.

Think About This

1. Can you think of some contemporary examples of people who have it all but whose lives reveal that having it all isn't all there is to life?

2. The Bible says that people live in the fear of death all their lives (Heb 2:15). Do you see any evidence that this is so? What about death makes people afraid?

3. Solomon is saying that, yes, we're going to die, but this is not a signal for us to go on a lifelong binge, as though somehow that were the meaning of life. He counsels contentment with our situation, diligence in all our opportunities and a heart of gratitude to God for what he gives us in life. What difference might it actually make if more people could learn to live like this?

4. The reason that people choose not to live this way is because of sin in their hearts. Solomon calls this "madness." What is sin? Do you think people are aware that there is such a thing as sin? Why or why not? How do they respond to it (or to their disbelief in it)?

5. Solomon says that the wisdom we need to succeed in life—that is, to find contentment and to appreciate the good gifts of God—cannot be found on an "under-the-sun" basis. People must learn to look to God, get to know him and his will, and trust his wisdom and counsel. Have you found this to be true in your life? Explain.

Man may possess splendid gifts and abilities to build up life,
but he cannot guarantee that he will be able to use them.
He may find himself at the mercy of events and occurrences
that can nullify his talents.
Man's accomplishments are not in strict accord
with the means he possesses within himself. . . .
Time and chance stand back of all man's work and govern his life
without his being able to control them.

MICHAEL KELLEY

Contentment is God's mandate for our lives. . . .
True contentment is an act of faith. It is a decision about our attitude
based on obedience to God's stated will.
God never sanctions discontent, for discontent is the denial
of faith, and without faith it is impossible to please God.

GORDON J. KEDDIE

STUDY 10

Qoheleth's point is to impress upon his readers
that foolishness should not be shrugged off as tolerable and harmless.
It is not "just one of those things" to be accepted as a normal
(and okay within limits) part of life.
Rather, we ought to be sensitive to the depth of the problem
and its far-reaching consequences. The reason there is
"no fool like an old fool," is that so many young fools
never change their ways!

GORDON J. KEDDIE

Read Ecclesiastes 10

In this chapter Solomon backs away from the larger philosophical framework, in which he has been arguing matters of life and death, into the earthy, mundane realities of daily living, where he appeals to common sense in his readers. He seems to suggest that if we can see certain obvious things so clearly, we should be able to grasp the greater reality that life under the sun will *never* make sense. Only an "under-the-heavens" perspective will satisfy men and women who know wisdom when they see it.

Think About This

1. Pick one or two of the situations Solomon relates in Ecclesiastes 10 and see if you can provide a contemporary example. What is the common sense notion each example indicates?

2. That many people often choose to set common sense aside and do what seems risky, improbable or even foolish is abundantly clear. Ecclesiastes 9 told us that the reason for this is sin in the human heart. In light of the fact that sin is powerful enough to override common sense and make us do what is foolish, how would you

explain what sin is? What is the danger of going through life without dealing with sin?

3. We don't hear much about sin these days. Why do you suppose this is so? What ideas do people substitute for the notion of sin?

4. If sin is a reality in us, as Solomon and the rest of the Bible declare, and if it has the ability (among other things) to override common sense and cause people to do foolish and destructive things, what does this suggest about humanity's ultimate need?

5. Solomon seems to be illustrating in this chapter what he stated succinctly in Proverbs 14:12:

> There is a way that seems right to a man,
>   but the ends thereof are the ways of death.

Think of some ways that people have tried, in their own effort, to overcome the problem of sin and all its effects. Where does each of these ways break down?

The pity is that the fool has no idea what he is talking about.
He has no idea what the future holds.
His unbelief and failure to consider that there is a future judgment,
wherein the totality of life will be reviewed,
puts him at such a huge disadvantage compared
to the devout, wise man that he is to be pitied.

WALTER KAISER

In some areas those who live without God are exceedingly wise.
But not when it comes to weighing up the meaning of life.
At this point they are at a loss as to what to say.
Their whole view is this-worldly and materialistic.
Their philosophy is ultimately one of despair.
Knowing death will soon rob them of everything they have
ever lived for, they wonder what the point of it all is.
Life is unsatisfying and meaningless. There is only one thing to do—
to live for the moment, for the here and now.

STUART OLYOTT

STUDY 11

He has shown us that the industrious inventiveness
of self-proclaimed autonomous man
to carve meaning for himself from life on planet Earth
is little more than the twitchings and spasms of spiritual death.
Interwoven throughout his exposition of meaninglessness
is an emergent tapestry of rising hope
that points to God's alternatives to man's prevailing predicament.
The last two chapters of Ecclesiastes call for decisions
to be God's disciples and to live in faith for him.

GORDON J. KEDDIE

Read Ecclesiastes 11

In a sense, Solomon's main message in this book is that you should do the best you can in life to be content, industrious, selfless and ready to capitalize on every opportunity. For if this life is all there is, then you should make the most of it while you can and not wear yourself out in vain hopes of finding some deep meaning or unfading wealth or glory. But if this life is *not* all there is, and if we are all going to stand before God some day, then you need to live this way out of gratitude to him and as a way of preparing to meet him in judgment. The difference, of course, is that this way makes sense and coheres with the natural order, whereas the other way makes no sense at all, hence the ongoing frustrations and disappointments of those who try to live it.

Think About This

1. Take a few moments to review your responses to questions from previous chapters. What does Solomon seem to be saying to you especially? Is he touching home at any points?

2. Look at the various illustrations and images in Ecclesiastes 11. Which of them

most appeals to you, describes you best or speaks to some hope or aspiration in your life? Why?

3. Do any of these illustrations or images stand as a rebuke to you at this time? Which ones, and in what way?

4. Do most people you know believe in a coming judgment before God? If not, what do they believe about what happens at death and afterward? How have they come to that conclusion? Does it make sense for them to pursue the lives they have chosen in the light of that view? Why or why not?

5. Do you agree with Solomon that the days of youth are vanity? Why or why not? What can be done about this?

The heart turned from its own way, and turned to God,
brings the substance of happiness, instead of the shadow—
the reality instead of the name. Youth devoted to sin is the saddest—
youth consecrated to God is the brightest—
object in a world of darkness and sorrow.

CHARLES BRIDGES

The world belongs to God, and He has granted you
the opportunity to build up life. Give yourself to life in all its
richness and fullness. If things seem perverse and distorted,
do not let that bother you. Rather, while you have strength
in your limbs and ambition in your souls,
put your talents and gifts to work. Life may not turn out
as you expect, but you must not permit its uncertainties
and disturbances to impair your energies.

MICHAEL KELLEY

STUDY 12

*The fear of God is a habit of mind which acknowledges him
at every step, and which views everything
in relation to him who is eternally holy, just and good.
It is not the degrading and demoralizing dread of his power
such as can be found in many pagan religions,
but an inward attitude which loves him, is aware that life
is lived in his presence and which longs to please him.
It nurses the sincere and heartfelt intention to live for him,
not for oneself, but for him!*

STUART OLYOTT

Read Ecclesiastes 12

Solomon brings his essay to an end, reiterating in no uncertain terms what he has only struck glancing blows at so far—that life consists in knowing God, in loving and obeying him, and not in any of the vain ideas that mere human beings may imagine as they seek to make sense of life under the sun.

Think About This

1. Polls consistently reveal that over 90 percent of all Americans believe in God. What are we to make of this, given the fact that our society continues to drift further and further from the moral posture that God requires of us (Mic 6:8)?

2. Do you think there is any value to this knowledge of God as a starting point to begin talking to people about the one true God? Explain.

3. Solomon strongly appeals to the reality and finality of death—and the judgment of God to follow—in seeking to turn his son from his wayward lifestyle. Do you think this is a legitimate way of approaching people today? Can you cite any biblical support for your answer?

4. Solomon may seem to despise learning in general, but that is certainly not the case. Rather, he means to insist that learning finds its ultimate value only in the light of the knowledge of God. How can you see this illustrated in Paul's address before the Greek philosophers in Acts 17:22-34? How should his example counsel us in our effort to help people come to know the one true God?

5. Solomon says his son is seeking the *way* to live, the *truth* about the meaning of life, and as full and rich a *life* as he can possibly know. Jesus claimed that he is *the* way, *the* truth, and *the* life, and that no one can ever hope to know God apart from him. Given the absoluteness of those statements, what are we to make of Jesus?

Youth, the years of bodily strength and mental alertness,
is the time to work not just for temporal rewards
but for everlasting fruit. It is not the time to wile away one's life
in a vain pursuit of bodily enticements
and trifling and dissipating gaiety.

M I C H A E L   K E L L E Y

Those who are oppressed by the meaninglessness of life
under the sun and see the emptiness of their lives
need desperately to remember the only one who can
redeem such lostness and fill up the caverns of our despair
with his everlasting love!

G O R D O N   J .   K E D D I E

Abbreviations

Commentaries

Bridges	Bridges, Charles. *Ecclesiastes*. 1860. Reprint, Edinburgh: Banner of Truth, 1992.
Kaiser	Kaiser, Walter. *Ecclesiastes: Total Life*. Chicago: Moody Press, 1979.
Keddie	Keddie, Gordon J. *Looking for the Good Life: The Search for Fulfillment in the Light of Ecclesiastes*. Phillipsburg, N.J.: Presbyterian & Reformed, 1991.
Kelley	Kelley, Michael. *The Burden of God: Studies in Wisdom and Civilization from the Book of Ecclesiastes*. Minneapolis: Contra Mundum, 1993.
Longman	Longman, Tremper, III. *The Book of Ecclesiastes*. The New International Commentary on the Old Testament. Grand Rapids, Mich.: Eerdmans, 1998.
Murphy	Murphy, Roland. *Ecclesiastes*. Word Biblical Commentary 23A. Dallas: Word, 1992.
Olyott	Olyott, Stuart. *A Life Worth Living and a Lord Worth Loving: Ecclesiastes and Song of Solomon*. Durham, U.K.: Evangelical Press, 1983.
Whybray	Whybray, R. N. *Ecclesiastes*. Century Bible Commentary. Grand Rapids, Mich.: Eerdmans, 1989.

Bible Versions

KJV	King James Version
MT	Masoretic Text
NASB	New American Standard Bible
NIV	New International Version
NKJV	New King James Version
Q	Qumran Text
RSV	Revised Standard Version

Notes

Introduction
ᵃSee the commentators cited in context in the discussions that follow, especially Keddie, Olyott and Bridges. The view I present in this book is also that of Dr. John Currid of Reformed Theological Seminary.

ᵇSee especially Keddie and Olyott on this section.

Chasing the Wind: Ecclesiastes 1
ᵃThe word *qoheleth*, which is variously translated "preacher" or "teacher," seems to derive from the verb *qahal*, which means "to assemble" (Kaiser 24-25). As a feminine participle it emphasizes the abstract element of the office or activity associated with the verb, and the writer intends for readers to think of him in those terms (Whybray 2). If we take the writer at his word and understand him to be Solomon (besides David, only Solomon was king over Israel in Jerusalem; Olyott 18; Kaiser 25-29), it would make sense for him to want us to think of him in this role rather than as king. Israel was beginning to attain the height of its greatness when Solomon led the people in worship of God on the day of the temple's dedication (1 Kings 8; 2 Chron 6; Longman 2), the day when God came down among them in all his glory. Solomon stood in the divine presence interceding for the people, commending them to God's care and officiating over the first sacrifices by which the people rededicated themselves to God and his covenant. It was a day of great rejoicing, followed by a brief time in which it appeared that Israel might actually fulfill the promise of God's calling upon them (see 1 Kings 10; cf. Gen 12:1-3). However, Solomon proved incapable of abiding in the Lord. He disgraced himself in the office of king, as he will show, and he may well have considered that a reminder of his work as worship leader would carry more weight as he led his readers to recall the days of his wisdom and Israel's glory, rather than their material wealth but spiritual decline during the latter years of his kingship (Bridges 2-3; Kaiser 31; cf. 1 Kings 11:1-4).

ᵇCompare NIV. Most other versions render this phrase, a superlative use of the genitive, as "vanity of vanities." For this translation, see Longman 61.

[c] This phrase provides an important qualifier in Solomon's argument, as the next note will show (cf. Longman 61-62). The question raised in this verse was especially relevant for Solomon, who had worked very hard but whose kingdom would, as he knew, be torn asunder because of his folly.

[d] In verses 3-11 Solomon undertakes a broad preliminary summary, in the most general terms, of his observations concerning life lived under the sun. By this phrase he means life lived only with reference to this material world, as though things, people, activities, experiences and the passage of time made up the only existence we can know (Olyott 22; Bridges 8, 10; Keddie 8). He will contrast this with life lived under the heavens, as we shall see. In this summary of his observations (vv. 4-11) Solomon touches on familiar areas to which people look for meaning—their work (v. 3), the generations of their families and of human history (v. 4), the processes of nature, that is, the natural sciences (vv. 5-7), and the details and distractions of everyday life (vv. 8-11). Solomon was on a quest for meaning, what Douglas John Hall has identified for our own generation as "the most gripping search of humanity in our context" (*The End of Christendom and the Future of Christianity* [Harrisburg, Penn.: Trinity Press International, 1997], p. 26). His conclusion, from a strictly secular perspective, is that there is nothing new, nothing of meaning and nothing to hope for, if life is nothing more than a temporal/material merry-go-around (Bridges 8; Keddie 5).

[e] Hebrew "stands forever."

[f] "Dumb," that is, in the sense that it yields no final answers for human seeking.

[g] "Verse 4 enunciated the principle that the earth remains the same despite the constant cycle of humans and nature" (Longman 68).

[h] Hebrew "is panting."

[i] Hebrew "all things are wearying."

[j] Hebrew "man is not able to speak."

[k] Hebrew "is not filled."

[l] As Whybray points out, Solomon is here "drawing attention to the parallel between nature and human nature in order to point out the limitations within which man will do well to be content to live his life as an integral part of the whole 'work of God'" (Whybray 45). This motif of contentment with what God gives us will constitute a major part of Solomon's advice to the reader. Contentment can lead to gratitude and the true knowledge of God, whereas ambition and self-seeking lead to idolatry, vanity and a life without lasting meaning or purpose.

[m] "Human beings of today are the same sinful human beings of the past, and thus there are no new developments or progress in the human race" (Longman 73).

[n] Hebrew "there is no remembrance of former things."

[o] He seems to be getting ahead of himself, so having made a brief introductory declamation, in what follows Solomon proceeds to tell his story in more detail. All his observations, experiences, possessions and achievements left him flat. In all these things he could find no concise, convincing elucidation of the meaning of life, why we are here,

what we're supposed to be doing, what is good or true or beautiful, what will last forever and what is merely temporal. Everything seemed utterly meaningless, a mere chasing after the wind (v. 14).

[p]The Hebrew will allow for this rendering of the perfect "I was." Cf. NASB, RSV.

[q]Whybray points out that Solomon "begins with a self-introduction, following a tradition of Near Eastern—especially Egyptian—wisdom literature in which an old man, sometimes a king or one who for literary purposes claims to be a king, draws on the experiences of a lifetime to give advice to his son or successor" (Whybray 48).

[r]Hebrew "set my heart."

[s]Hebrew "an evil matter"; KJV "sore travail"; RSV "unhappy business"; NASB "grievous task"; NIV "heavy burden."

[t]Hebrew "afflict." Cf. RSV.

[u]Recognizing his inexperience, Solomon, at the beginning of his reign as king of Israel, asked the Lord to give him wisdom so that he might understand the needs of his people and rule them in a way that would be pleasing to God and a source of blessing for them (1 Kings 3:6-9). Here in Ecclesiastes he tells us what is only hinted at in 1 Kings 3: that the wisdom he would need would come from much study and contemplation of life in God's world (Kelley 73). This would not be an easy task, as he says in the last part of verse 13 (Keddie 15-16; Kelley 74). However, it is a task that God has appointed to human beings. If people want to know God and to experience the fullness of life as he intends, they will have to put their minds to the study of what he has been pleased to reveal of himself and his wisdom, both in the creation around us and in his Word (Kelley 74). In order to know the fullness of life as God intends, people must gain wisdom from him, must learn to look at life not merely under the sun but under the heavens, that is, from God's vantage point—the vantage point of the eternal, uncreated Deity who, having made the world and everything in it, alone understands perfectly how it is to be enjoyed (Kelley 74). Solomon wished to rule well, so he set a course of studying life as God intended it to be lived, to gain the wisdom he would need to make sense out of the multiplicity of situations, needs and opportunities that would come his way as king.

[v]Remember, he set out seeking to learn "under the heavens," that is, with a view to understanding life as God intends it. He ended up seeing everything under the sun, that is, from a strictly secular perspective, and he found life to be meaningless in that light.

[w]He was, after all, David's son, and had grown up in a household torn and troubled by the consequences of David's times of wandering from the Lord.

[x]In the rhyming paraphrase I have chosen at times to use "feeding on the wind" when Solomon says "chasing the wind." This allows opportunity to dramatize the vanity of that which the world serves up apart from God. The meaning remains essentially the same. In fact, the Hebrew verb *raghut*, meaning "to graze or feed," is a cognate of the noun RAGHUT, "chasing." In the infinitive construct of the verb the forms are the same.

[y]Solomon started out trying to see things God's way, trying to understand his life and calling according to God's plan and purpose. Somewhere along the line, however, in the

midst of all his study and activity, he lost sight of his goal, strayed from his perspective and began looking at things from the point of view of a this-worldly experience (Bridges 18). We know that Solomon took many foreign wives (1 Kings 11:1), undoubtedly because his studies showed that this was the way to build stable relationships with neighboring kingdoms. Yes, God's Word had warned against this practice, even forbidden it (1 Kings 11:2); but after all, Solomon was a modern monarch, and he may have reasoned that the times demanded a dif-

ferent course of him. His many marriages led to idolatry (1 Kings 11:3-4), which is in every case a turning away from devotion to the one true God to following various false deities, all of which, in the end, are nothing more than the creations of human minds. Somewhere in this process Solomon lost his bearings. Pragmatism and expediency replaced the search for wisdom; political power, sensual experience and materialism began to be his overwhelming concerns; and as we shall see, he drifted from one experience, perspective, philosophy or achievement to the next, looking for what he hoped would make sense out of it all and enable him to rule wisely, only to be disappointed by what he observed under the sun. The rest of chapter 1 and most of chapter 2 record his experiences and reflections during the time of his wandering from the path God had set for him and trying to make sense out of his life apart from God. The remainder of the book will assert the necessity of knowing and serving God, resting by faith in him, if life is to make sense and be worthwhile.

²Hebrew "be counted."

ᵃᵃSolomon will develop this point more fully in chapter 4.

ᵇᵇHere we can see how Solomon's mind was working. Although he had begun to turn away from God, still he was looking for solutions to the problems that faced him as ruler of a growing nation—problems of justice, deprivation and civil order (Bridges 21-22). But the strictly secular perspective into which he had drifted provided no certain ways of dealing with such matters. Who is to say what's right or wrong when no eternal values are acknowledged?

ᶜᶜHebrew "heart." The use of heart here, where we would normally use mind, indicates involvement of Solomon's whole being, rather than mere intellectual curiosity.

ᵈᵈThe Hebrew verb tense allows the past perfect rendering.

ᵉᵉHebrew "I have come to know."

ᶠᶠIs Solomon's conscience piquing him a bit here? He says he set out to learn as much as he could about wisdom. But in retrospect he has to admit that he delved deeply into folly and madness as well—wine, women and song, as it were. He had become as expert in the one as in the other, and both, in the absence of a divine perspective, were empty, unsatisfying and lacking in meaning.

ᵍᵍHebrew "vexation."

ʰʰThroughout this book Solomon will commend the ways of wisdom to his readers. But he does not imply that becoming wise eliminates all the problems of life in society with other people (Bridges 23). In some ways gaining wisdom can make those problems seem worse: it adds a backdrop of truth against which to observe the foolish and self-destructive ways of those who refuse to consider God's purpose and plan. So, he seems to be implying, if only by way of thinking out loud, let's not make the mistake of equating wisdom with complete and perfect happiness in this life. The meaning of life is deeper than mere happiness, and the end of wisdom is not simply self-satisfaction.

Hating Life: Ecclesiastes 2

[a]This phrase is sort of the Hebrew equivalent to "Let the good times roll!" Most translations follow a suggested emendation of the Hebrew verb *nasach*, "to anoint," yielding the translation "to test" or "to prove." This does not strike me as necessary and even takes away from the image that Solomon wants to create, of literally drenching himself in revelry. Early in his reign, as he began his quest for wisdom and the meaning of life, his court was marked by massive indulgences (1 Kings 4:2-23). These seem to have been relatively harmless at the time, the expression perhaps of initial euphoria upon Solomon's ascendancy; however, it appears that from Solomon's perspective they may have been pursued to excess: "With what hilarity and laughter must the palace halls have echoed as Solomon, his courtiers, and his guests exchanged jokes, drank wine, listened to the witty merrymakers from all over the region, and feasted bountifully" (Kaiser 55).

[b]Hebrew "my heart leading in wisdom."

[c]The Hebrew demonstrative pronoun seems to point back to revelry as the subject of the verb following.

[d]Hebrew "if this might be good for the sons of men, what they might do under the sun the number of the days of their lives."

[e]Hebrew "made myself great of works."

[f]There were no doubt many in Solomon's retinue who would have preferred to continue the revelry for an indefinite time. Solomon seems quickly to have wearied of this diversion and chose instead to get on with more productive activities (1 Kings 5—7).

[g]This was perhaps how Solomon rationalized his many projects. "Creativity has to it an aura of public service. Any potential for self-indulgence can be balanced by a countervailing motive of altruism and a sense of lasting contribution to the common good" (Keddie 20).

[h]First Kings 10:23-25 indicates that foreign nations sent their treasures to Solomon as gifts in recognition of his greatness.

[i]The Hebrew is unclear at this point, although the root of this genitival construction may refer to the female breast. It appears to be a euphemism, perhaps even a slang term, for sexual liaisons. This is supported by the report of Solomon's actions in 1 Kings 11:1-4 and the translations of most versions except KJV and NKJV (Longman 92). As Whybray notes, the context would certainly seem to encourage this translation (Whybray 54).

[j]"Once again, as in 2:3, Qoheleth maintains that he remained wise even as he indulged in his pleasure" (Longman 93).

[k]Hebrew "under the sun."

[l]Solomon's consternation derives from his having been distracted from pursuing these works under the heavens and working at them instead under the sun. God had

commissioned him to rule the nation in wisdom and to find his own joy and satisfaction in knowing and serving the Lord. His brief fling with revelry may have sidetracked him so that he began looking to his work and accomplishments to give him a sense of purpose and well-being. He had, in short, made idols of his many projects. Each one satisfied while it was in process and for a time once it was completed. After a while, however, there was no more satisfaction in these works—even though they were magnificent and beautiful—than there was in revelry. Having lost his proper perspective, he lost any abiding sense of peace and fulfillment, which, as he will tell us, comes only from knowing and serving the Lord.

[m]Hebrew "he." Solomon seems to be thinking more about the generations to come than about one specific descendant, although he uses the singular. At the same time this could be a rather thinly veiled warning to his own son.

[n]Hebrew "the wise man's eyes are in his head." Solomon "is concerned simply to record the common experience of daily life in which common sense is an asset which some people lack" (Whybray 58).

[o]Hebrew "he goes about in darkness."

[p]He suggests the emptiness of a purely relativistic ethic. Richard Rorty and other postmodern thinkers espouse a wide range of life options, apart from any final authority to give guidance or definition. Rorty writes, "No past achievement, not Plato's or Christ's, can tell us about the ultimate significance of human life. No such achievement can give us a template on which to model our future. The future will widen endlessly. . . . The moral we should draw from the European past, and in particular from Christianity, is not instruction about the authority under which we should live, but suggestions about how to make ourselves wonderfully different from anything that has been" (*Achieving Our Country* [Cambridge, Mass.: Harvard University Press, 1998], p. 24). But if any way of life is as true and as good as every other, then they are all meaningful only to individuals, and therefore equally meaningless as explanations of life. Hence it makes no more sense to choose one than another or to exclude any aspect of all of them. All the relativist can say is that his chosen way of life is good for him; he cannot say it is the best life he could choose, or even that it could be considered true in any abiding sense, much less true or good for anyone else. Solomon sees this in a glance.

[q]This is the first mention of the theme of the tyranny of death over secular humankind (vv. 14-16).

[r]Hebrew "so I turned to hopelessness in my heart." NASB "completely despaired."

[s]Obviously everything in italics is implied. Solomon seems to be making the point that follows from an under-the-sun perspective.

[t]Hebrew "cause your soul to see good in your work." Cf. NASB. Solomon's point is that if work and the good life are all people can expect under the sun, then they had better make the most of it (Longman 106; Murphy 27).

[u]Solomon ultimately emerged from the views he arrived at under the sun. Here he invites

the reader to consider his more mature conclusions, which he will declare more forthrightly in chapters 11 and 12. He is speaking under the heavens in what follows.

ᵛHebrew "without me" (MT). A variant reading has "without him," which, following the reasoning in the next verse, seems to suggest the translation above. This simple scribal error can probably be attributed to a miscopying of a poorly written Hebrew letter, since *yod* and *vav* are similar in appearance.

Eternity in Our Hearts: Ecclesiastes 3

ᵃ"Matter" is accurate and seems to embrace more than "activity" (NIV), "event" (NASB) or "purpose" (KJV). Cf. RSV.

ᵇChapter 3 is the heart of Solomon's argument. Life makes sense only when it is lived "under the heavens," that is, with an eye to God's final control and authority and in a reverent, trustful relationship with him. Everything has its place in God's plan and economy, even though we humans cannot expect to understand it all perfectly. We must learn to live by faith, to trust in God's goodness and wisdom, and to be content with whatever he is pleased to bring to us in life. Thus we will find our truest happiness and highest sense of meaning and purpose (Whybray 68; Murphy 32).

ᶜ*Economy* is a formal theological term that refers to God's administration of everything according to his eternal plan and wise counsel and toward his redemptive purposes.

ᵈHebrew "to perish."

ᵉSolomon restates the question. Compare the way Job restates the questions God put in his reproach: Job 38:1-3; 42:3-4.

ᶠSolomon is thinking back on his initial mandate, as he expressed it in Ecclesiastes 1:12-13. While he strayed from this purpose, as we have seen, ultimately—and this is his point—he found his way back to a proper perspective, and it is this perspective which he urges on the reader in this section.

ᵍEcclesiastes 1:3; 2:24.

ʰPaul tells us that God has so made us that as we look at the world around us, we cannot help but see him in it and know that he is God and ought to be worshiped and served. On the day that God judges all people, none will be able to plead, "I did not know" (see Rom 1:20).

ⁱOtherwise where would be the need for faith, without which it is impossible to please God (Heb 11:6)?

ʲ"The pursuit of God-centered and God-honoring happiness, enjoyment of good food and drink, a zeal for doing good to all men, and satisfaction in one's work—all are legitimate goals for God's people. They are his gifts" (Keddie 35; cf. Bridges 69-71).

ᵏSee note q on chapter 12 for what it means to "fear" God.

ˡThis is essentially Paul's argument in Romans 1:18-21: the visible things of the creation are given so as to reveal the existence of God, so that all people will seek him. Paul makes the same point in his sermons in Acts 14 (v. 17) and 17 (vv. 26-27).

ᵐHebrew "God seeks what has been done." This insight, this awareness of recurrent patterns in nature, among certain Renaissance and post-Renaissance natural scientists, gave rise to the scientific revolution. See Steven Shapin, *The Scientific Revolution* (Chicago: University of Chicago Press, 1996), pp. 59-78.

[n]Bridges , p. 73.

[o]This is precisely the place that many scientists and theologians are arriving at today as they propose new theories of rationality and design to explain the origins of the cosmos. See the special section of *Touchstone* 12, no. 4 (July-August 1999).

[p]Ecclesiastes 1:15. Cf. Kelley 89.

[q]Solomon says virtually the same thing in Proverbs 18:4.

[r]Hebrew "I said in my heart."

[s]In fact, this is exactly the argument of many animal rights groups.

[t]And this is the response to animal rights groups of those who know that somehow humanity is different from, even above, the animals, although they may not know why or in what way.

[u]Here I am reminded of two remarks by the late Carl Sagan, a leading apologist for the evolutionary worldview: "I am a collection of water, calcium and organic molecules called Carl Sagan. You are a collection of almost identical molecules with a different collective label. But is that all? Is there nothing in here but molecules? Some people find this idea somehow demeaning to human dignity. For myself, I find it elevating that our universe permits the evolution of molecular machines as intricate and subtle as we" (*Cosmos* [New York: Random House, 1980], p. 127); "We live on a fragile planet, whose thoughtful preservation is essential if our children are to have a future. We are only custodians for a moment of a world that is itself no more than a mote of dust in a universe incomprehensively vast and old" (*Comet* [New York: Random House, 1985], p. 367). Yet if in the end human beings are mere dust, then the grave is all they can expect at the end of life. This hardly provides sufficient motivation for pursuing the lofty goals and high responsibility that Sagan encourages. Notice as well the inevitable way Sagan attributes personality to a universe that "permits" us to be what we are and that requires our custodianship.

[v]"Man looks beyond everyday occurrences and asks the meaning of them all. This is because he is a spiritual creature" (Olyott 28).

[w]Under the sun, that is.

[x]If the secular life, that is, life apart from God, is all there is, and if we are determined to be happy, then we had better learn to make the most of whatever our lot in life may be, for we cannot know whether there may something better beyond the grave. Under the sun—that is, from a strictly secular perspective—this kind of life is all anyone can expect. We need to make the most of it, pain and all.

[y]Solomon's conclusion is reflected in Steve Kowit's poem "Notice" (in *A Book of Luminous Things*, ed. Czeslaw Milosz [New York: Harcourt Brace, 1996], p. 199):

> This evening, the sturdy Levis

I wore every day for over a year
& which seemed to the end in perfect condition,
suddenly tore.
How or why I don't know,
but there it was—a big rip at the crotch.
A month ago my friend Nick
walked off a racquetball court,
showered,
got into his street clothes,
& halfway home collapsed & died.
Take heed you who read this
& drop to your knees now & again
like the poet Christopher Smart
& kiss the earth & be joyful
& make much of your time
& be kindly to everyone,
even to those who do not deserve it.
For although you may not believe it will happen,
you too will one day be gone.
I, whose Levis ripped at the crotch
for no reason,
assure you that such is the case.
Pass it on.

No One to Comfort Them: Ecclesiastes 4

[a]Keddie's summary of Solomon's argument to this point is extremely helpful:

> In the first three chapters, he sets the scene by surveying the general contours of our human predicament and the concomitant issues with which we must grapple in order to make sense and success of our lives. He spoke of the spiritual bankruptcy of secular, under-the-sun living (1:1-2:23). By way of contrast, he pointed briefly to the alternative, the life of faith in God (2:24-26). Finally, he argued for the certainties of God's providence and final judgment, urging, by implication, the necessity of receiving and enjoying life as the gift of God (3:1-22).
> The next seven chapters (4:1-10:20) flesh out this thesis by high-lighting particular problems and pointing to the Lord's answers. The recurring twin themes are, on the one hand, the utter emptiness of worldly values and, on the other hand, the meaning and joy that is to be found exclusively in a living faith relationship to God. (Keddie 42)

[b]The words for "oppressions" and "oppressed" here are the same word in the Hebrew. Their juxtaposition serves to emphasize the sad condition of those who suffer from the various injustices foisted on them by oppressors—whether vicious others, well-meaning but misguided teachers, selfish friends or constituents, or even themselves.
[c]"We make men without chests and expect of them virtue and enterprise. We laugh at

honour and are shocked to find traitors in our midst. We castrate and bid the geldings be fruitful" (C. S. Lewis, *The Abolition of Man* [New York: Macmillan, 1965], p. 35).

[d]Hebrew "there was one, and not another."

[e]Hebrew "his eyes were never full of riches."

[f]"The man of covetousness would keep his money within his last grasp. . . . Comfort, peace, usefulness, and—what is infinitely more important—the interests of the immortal soul—all is sacrificed to this mean and sordid lust" (Bridges 88). The implication in NASB and KJV that the man never asked himself this question is not supported by the context.

[g]"These verses have a common theme: it is dangerous and unwise for the individual to attempt to face life alone, and simple common sense to see the co-operation of others in all that one does" (Whybray 86).

[h]Hebrew "they fall," implying either one.

[i]The context seems to imply the marital relationship, although that is not the only possible interpretation.

[j]This construction appears to add faithful friendships to the benefit of a happy marriage.

[k]See previous note.

[l]Hebrew "who does not know to be enlightened."

[m]Again, Solomon emphasizes that what he is observing is the behavior of people who live under the sun, that is, without any absolute or transcendent values.

[n]"Each generation longs for a political messiah to usher in paradise" (Kelley 93).

[o]Solomon, it seems, is eager to avoid the fate that befell the great Ozymandias, as recorded by Percy Bysshe Shelley (in *The Top 500 Poems*, ed. Willam Harmon [New York: Columbia University Press, 1992], p. 495):

> I met a traveler from an antique land
> Who said: Two vast and trunkless legs of stone
> Stand in the desert. Near them, on the sand,
> Half sunk, a shattered visage lies, whose frown,
> And wrinkled lip, and sneer of cold command,
> Tell that its sculptor well those passions read
> Which yet survive, stamped on these lifeless things,
> The hand that mocked them and the heart that fed;
> And on the pedestal these words appear:
> "My name is Ozymandias, king of kings:
> Look on my works, ye Mighty, and despair!"
> Nothing beside remains. Round the decay
> Of that colossal wreck, boundless and bare
> The lone and level sands stretch far away.

Honest to God: Ecclesiastes 5

[a]"There is a self-evident hollowness in much of what passes for Christianity in this world

of ours" (Keddie 54).

[b]"Foolish minds think that God may be worshipped just as they please, but that is not the case. We should worship him as he himself has specified, and should remember that not to do so is sin" (Olyott 37).

[c]Ecclesiastes 4:17 in the Hebrew.

[d]"Above all else, do 'go to the house of God' (5:1) with a receptive attitude and a readiness to listen rather than lecture God on what He ought to do" (Kaiser 74).

[e]Commentators struggle with the sense of this strange construction. It seems to say something like this: When you have a lot on your mind you dream a lot, but dreams are empty reality. So too the fool: When he speaks a lot it only proves that he is a fool, for his words, though they be ever so many, mean nothing.

[f]"He wants to distinguish an empty, meaningless religion from the real thing. He wants to root out formalism and come to experience living communion with the Lord" (Keddie 55).

[g]Keep in mind that in biblical terminology a fool is one who has no true, saving faith in God (Ps 14:1). Those who make vows frivolously and then do not keep them are very much like fools, playing at religion rather than exercising true faith.

[h]The messenger here is probably the local religious authority—we would say the local pastor. The intention seems to be that when our pastor calls on us to fulfill some vow we have made to the Lord, we should not say that we didn't really mean it and shouldn't have made the vow in the first place, or that making the vow was a mistake. Cf. Longman 154.

[i]Solomon now turns his focus to dishonesty on the part of rulers.

[j]"Secular man especially cannot engineer a social project which comports with his ideals of justice and equity, because he lacks a genuine transcendent authority principle solely within his own conscience that is sufficient to offset the centrifugal force inherent in every man obeying the voice of ambition (or avarice, covetousness, indolence, intemperance, etc.)" (Kelley 98).

[k]Solomon is describing "ascending tiers of officialdom at once fobbing off the pleading victim and passing on a share of the loot to shifty-eyed superiors" (Keddie 66). Cf. Bridges 110; Whybray 97.

[l]The translation follows the NASB, treating the niphal form of the verb in a middle or reflexive sense. As Longman notes, this is a very difficult verse to translate. However, the use of the preposition *to* rather than *from* with fields suggests the position taken by the NASB (Longman 158-59). What the verse proposes, however, does not usually happen, so the oppression of the people increases.

[m]Hebrew "silver."

[n]In this section Solomon's theme appears to be that wealth, or the pursuit of it, makes it difficult for us to be honest with ourselves or others. It is just another source of vanity in a life without God.

[o]That is, whether hangers-on who seek some favor from the wealthy, or those to whom

the wealthy, because of their conspicuous consumption, pay out their money. [p]"As one's means increase, so do 'bills'" (Longman 165).

[q]Here Solomon foreshadows a theme he will elaborate more fully in verses 18-20 and in later chapters: the value of learning contentment so as not to allow riches, or the desire for them, to become a source of oppression.

[r]Solomon condemns hoarding. Wealth is given in order to be put to good use, doing good for oneself and others as a wise steward over what God has entrusted to one. Hoarding wealth— merely stashing it away with no intention of using it as God intends—is therefore a great evil indeed.

[s]Keddie 69.

[t]I take this to imply the darkness of spiritual ignorance, of being unable, in spite of our labors or our wealth, to make sense of life under the sun—apart from faith in God.

[u]Under the sun the most a person can hope for is to take what life gives and be content. Don't seek more, and don't complain about what you don't have. It may be that in the state of contentment, one will come to see one's life as basically good and recognize the good things as gifts from God. This may then set the person on the course of seeking God (Lk 3:14; Acts 14:17; 17:24-27; Jas 1:17-18). Thus coming to know the Giver of every good and perfect gift, one may find more than contentment. Such a one may find real peace and joy and come to understand the meaning and purpose of life within the divine economy. God's involvement in this process, as implied in the verse, should be understood as permissive. He allows people to follow their lusts into all manner of worldly distractions.

[v]Compare 2 Corinthians 4:3-4, where the phrase "god of this world" may be taken epexegetically: "the god that consists of this world." People become so distracted by the things of this world, so attached to created things, that they devote their energies to attaining, enjoying, preserving and increasing these, leaving themselves little time or inclination to think about God (Rom 1:18-21). Instead of allowing their contentment to lead them to gratitude and the quest to know God, the Giver of good gifts, they in effect make idols out of things and devote themselves to these, to their own hurt (Rom 1:22-32). This too, as Solomon would say, is vanity and chasing after the wind.

Full Lives, Empty Souls: Ecclesiastes 6

[a]Hebrew "it is great upon men." KJV "it is common"; NASB "it is prevalent."

[b]Solomon emphasizes throughout this book the divine prerogative to dispose of wealth as God sees fit. If people understood and accepted that God is pleased to give them however much or little they possess, they might learn to see their lot in life as good, thanking him for all his gifts, be they meager or much, and contenting themselves with his goodness. They do not generally; instead they make idols out of things and embark on a tireless quest to get more and more. Solomon's point is that when people fail to acknowledge God's goodness to them, when they fail to live in contentment and thanksgiving, which could lead to the knowledge of God (Acts 17:26-27; Rom 1:21), they

follow instead their fleshly lusts and ambitions and make idols out of all manner of created things, hoping in them to find the happiness and meaning they seek (Rom 1:22-25).

ᶜSolomon's point is that "a man may possess wealth, honor, numerous children, long life, and virtually every outward good that anyone could possibly imagine; yet he can still be a very broken, dissatisfied, and unhappy person" (Kaiser 80).

ᵈCf. Keddie 72.

ᵉHebrew "it knows resting to this one more than that one."

ᶠCf. Longman 171.

ᵍHebrew "see." NIV "fails to enjoy."

ʰHebrew "all the man's work is for his mouth."

ⁱHebrew "what remains to the wise man more than to the fool?"

ʲHebrew "to walk."

ᵏHebrew "the going-of-good-the soul," that is, the soul's pursuit of its own ends and means. In Hebrew this is expressly intended as one idea, the two words joined in verb-object order by *maqqeph*. The way I have rendered it captures better the essence of what is intended. NIV "appetite" and RSV and KJV "desire" seem to me to obscure the point.

ˡHebrew "that which is its name is already called."

ᵐThis is an important verse. Most commentators want to see the contracted relative pronoun as referring to God, who is stronger than humankind. However, it is also possible to take this as pointing to a truth that is known but denied: that people were made for God. "Mortal man, the creation of God, cannot set aside or overcome that divinely established connection between earthly things and the dissatisfaction with those things apart from God" (Kaiser 81). The reference may well be to the sense of God that every person has by virtue of having been created in his image (cf. 3:11). Human beings have always known that they are more than merely material beings, that they have some connection with transcendent reality. This is why there has never been a civilization devoid of religion of some sort. People know they connect with that which is beyond the merely physical, and they continually strive to make contact with it. At the same time, Solomon seems to be saying, they try to live as if this were not so, feeding their fleshly and material needs to the neglect of their souls, as though somehow their souls did not matter. Yet they cannot get away from it. Indeed, humankind's "original dignity only serves to set out more vividly [its] present degradation" (Bridges 129). The sense that people have spiritual needs is stronger than their passion for fleshly gratification, and it drives them either to seek God or to fall into idolatry of some form. Solomon dismisses all the idolatrous diversions that people cling to in their under-the-sun existence as "vanity and chasing after the wind."

ⁿ"Strange delusion, to suppose that more of this world would bring increase of happiness!" (Bridges 126)

ᵒHebrew "for there are many words increasing vanity."

ᵖThis can be seen as a reference to contemporary worldviews, which seek, generally apart from any metaphysical convictions, to make sense of life under the sun. Solomon says it has been of no profit. He continues to insist that no matter how many words are proffered in explanation of the secular life, it will not make sense to human beings, who know implicitly that they are spiritual beings.

[q]"The metaphor is one that highlights the brevity of human life, but perhaps even more pointedly its ephemerality. It conveys the fact that humans are so ephemeral, so insubstantial, that they are unable to know the future, what happens after they leave the scene" (Longman 178). "Both the opaqueness and the transient character of the shadow are the point of comparison" (Murphy 58).

Going to Extremes: Ecclesiastes 7

[a]"By means of a series of contrasts the Preacher makes clear that some things in life hold greater importance than other things" (Kelley 113). "A heap of paradoxes are rising before us, like the beatitudes which preface the Sermon on the Mount. But the paradoxes of the Bible open out valuable truths" (Bridges 135).

[b]The "good ointment" or "fine oil" was an expensive commodity that, when worn, suggested the wealth and status of the wearer. As such, it was superficial adornment, especially when compared with the lasting benefit of a good reputation. The warning here is against superficiality in place of character.

[c]Some commentators believe that Solomon was commending death as a final way out of all life's foolishness and oppression. However, given the ultimately positive message of the book and Solomon's desire to provide correct instruction for living "under the heavens," the interpretation I have followed seems to make more sense: that people ought to seek to establish a wise and good lifestyle, characterized by contentment and gratitude in the knowledge of God, so that at the end of life they will have something worthwhile to leave behind. "When a person is born you can only measure his life in terms of its potential. When he dies, you can look back on what he has actually accomplished" (Olyott 47).

[d]Most commentators seem to focus on the "house of mourning" as more desirable for the lessons mourning can teach us about the shortness of life and the fact that death is the great equalizer, after which comes the judgment. I have no basic problem with this view, except that it does not contrast with the self-seeking ways of the fool as well as what I am suggesting.

[e]"To learn from the past is good, as is the desire for the fullness of God's blessing now and in the future. But to pine after the past is to attempt to live life in reverse. Your real life is now and in the future. Your experience, past and present, must drive you forward to seek the Lord's blessing in the application of lessons learned, not backward to embittered dreams of vanished joy" (Keddie 86).

[f]Neither Solomon nor the Scriptures in general denounce wealth. Rather, wealth must always be combined with the kind of wisdom that shows compassion for people's needs and allows us to be good stewards of God's gracious gifts.

[g]Most translations render this "but the advantage of knowledge is that wisdom," where "is that" is understood by the context. I see no need to insert the understood stative verb at this point. The genetival construction can be translated as I have rendered it and seems to make more sense, since *knowledge* agrees with the feminine form of the verb, as well as *wisdom*.

[h]Even though we might very much like to, especially some of those "crooked places" (1:15) God throws in our path from time to time. Solomon will counsel that we must learn to accept these, as well as the good things God gives us, with contentment, gratitude and trust.

[i]That is, the uncertainties of life allow God to be God and human beings to be human beings. God is the Giver of whatever he pleases; people are to receive it all with gratitude and contentment, knowing it comes from a good God. For one to be able with complete accuracy to predict one's future, based on one's works or desires, would be to rob God of his divine prerogative and to take away the necessity of faith, without which it is impossible to please God (Heb 11:6). Cf. Longman 192.

[j]In what follows we should see Solomon reasoning ironically, under the sun as it were, as he reflects on the truth of verse 15.

[k]Most commentators see *wisdom* and *righteousness* in these verses as the pretension of these virtues. This strikes me as rather hard to justify from the immediate context. As Solomon seems to move freely between the under-the-sun and under-the-heavens perspectives, it makes more sense to me to see him reflecting as a secular man might, saying to himself, Well, then, if being wise and righteous doesn't guard against the experience of evil, why bother? Cf. Olyott 50.

[l]Solomon "is saying here that there is enough wickedness clinging to our souls without giving ourselves over to it!" (Keddie 95).

[m]Hebrew "for." I have translated it "however," a legitimate translation as it seems to me that Solomon offers this verse as a caution against what he says in verse 19, consistent with what he said in verse 16. People should not think that in pursuing wisdom as an end in itself—that is, apart from the knowledge of God—they will attain a condition of sinlessness.

[n]"Even among the faithful sin can, and often does, gain the upper hand. It is a reminder that the 'crookedness' in man is an ever present problem, which he is powerless to solve on his own" (Kelley 117).

[o]Cf. Keddie 95.

[p]The interpretation given in the verse narrative assumes that Solomon is referring to himself and his coming to the realization that there was no wisdom to be found in continuing to add women—for him, the symbol of life under the sun—to his life. He already had a thousand women—three hundred wives and seven hundred concubines (1 Kings 11:3)—and none of them had shown him the way to a contented soul. Cf. Bridges 177-78.

Civic Wisdom: Ecclesiastes 8

[a]Commentators disagree over where this verse fits in the overall narrative, whether as an introduction to this section or a conclusion to the previous one. My view is that Solomon is doing what he occasionally does elsewhere in this book: asserting his role as one who, having experienced the vanity of secular life, has now come to a better understanding of the ways of human beings before God. Here, therefore, he is indirectly urging the reader to pay attention to his conclusions by alluding to himself as the wise man whose mind and life have been changed, which any of his contemporaries could have confirmed.

[b]"Knowing the Lord softens facial features as much as it melts the hardness of the heart" (Keddie 99-100). "One display of this Divine transformation may be seen in the change of the boldness of our face. Once it was hard and stern loftiness. Now, without losing one atom of its firmness, it melts down into humility" (Bridges 184). "Wisdom changes the unpleasant appearance of a person" (Murphy 82).

[c]The Hebrew can mean either "keep" or "guard." I prefer the latter because it seems more to involve one's inner heart attitude than a mere outward keeping might suggest.

[d]Hebrew "oath of God." Whether this is an objective genitive—the oath taken to God—or a subjective genitive—the oath God has taken to support the king—is debated by commentators. However, the difference between these does not dramatically affect the interpretation. It may have been that in ancient Israelite society some kind of oath was taken upon the ascension of a new king—for example, the use of a psalm such as Psalm 2 to mark his coronation. This is what may be in view here. If so, it is somewhat analogous to the American pledge of allegiance (Keddie 104; cf. also Whybray 130).

[e]Solomon is talking about earthly rulers here; however, as the end of this chapter makes clear, he also has in mind the divine King, against whom no one can stand. If it is the part of wisdom to heed the words of earthly rulers and be very reluctant to rebel against them, how much more should we honor and obey the word of God? Cf. Kelley 124-25 and Keddie 104, 195.

[f]That is, as if demanding an explanation or presuming to hold the king accountable. Note the way Job 9:12 addresses this same question with respect to God.

[g]"Those who do obey the king will avoid unpleasant consequences" (Longman 213).

[h]Commentators differ on whether to translate the Hebrew *ruach*, as "wind" or "spirit," since it is amenable to both, and since Solomon uses it both ways in this book. I have chosen "wind" to keep consistency with the theme of chasing after the wind, the futility of seeking an understanding of life apart from God.

[i]In Israelite society, when the nation came under attack all men of fighting age were called to war, with just a few carefully spelled-out exceptions (Deut 20).

[j]Some commentators want to emend the verb here from "to bury" to "to draw near," which is done in the Hebrew by reversing the order of the last two consonants. The consequent interpretation allows them to envision the wicked as going in and out of the temple merely to be seen doing so. I do not believe this emendation is justified and have

chosen to let the text stand as is.

^kThat is, their wicked deeds.

^l"Mark the emphasis of this presumptuous sin. The heart—as if it were but one common heart of the sons of men—is bent on one purpose acting in every man in the world— this heart is set—fully set—it is not yielding to sin under some special assault, but one wilful—habitual—determined resolution—without remorse—all—to do evil" (Bridges 198).

^mThe syntax allows a question, and the context, given the remark in verse 12, suggests it. The point seems to be that although the evil person's life may be long, it is ephemeral, like a shadow. Cf. 6:12.

ⁿ"Most commentators have rightly seen that the sleeplessness referred to here is connected with man's unceasing but fruitless attempt by the exercise of wisdom to understand the ways of God" (Whybray 138).

Alive (at Least): Ecclesiastes 9

^aKeddie offers another useful summary at this point: "Ecclesiastes lays out for us the consequences of forgetting what it means to be truly human. A thread of delicious irony is woven very deftly through the presentation of this theme. It is the notion that when man sees his humanness exclusively as an under-the-sun (secular, godless) humanism, he actually loses the essential perspective that defines both who he is and what constitutes his true calling and destiny. Denying the wisdom of God and his relationship to him as the creature to his Creator, he embraces the very opposite—under-the-sun meaninglessness—as the conventional wisdom for the new humanity, independent of God and alone in the universe. Qoheleth is therefore at pains to remind us of our human frailty and our need to depend upon the Lord" (Keddie 127).

^bMany commentators, understanding Ecclesiastes to have been written much later than Solomon's day, see this word as an Aramaic noun. The pointing suggests this may be so. However, the radicals are the normal Hebrew ones for "servants, " a word which would have been quite familiar to Solomon. I take the construction as indicating the whole gamut of social roles, from those most admired to those generally most despised.

^c"For him 'the hand of God' is not a consoling thought or a sign of predilection; it merely designates divine power, from which there is no escape" (Murphy 90).

^d"The general sense of the verse is reasonably clear: God controls men's lives absolutely, and men are left in ignorance of what is going on" (Whybray 141). This, however, is not a summons to despair but an injunction to learn to know and trust in God.

^eSeveral commentators want to see this as referring to the taking of oaths or vows. I follow Kaiser (and others) in holding that it indicates "profane swearers" (Kaiser 96).

^fMost translations and commentators follow the Q variant of this word, "is joined." However, given Solomon's comment in verse 1 about God's sovereignty, the verb in the MT as I have translated it seems more to the point. See notes c and d.

^g"The short proverb that ends the verse makes it clear that Qoheleth is favoring life over

death here, but it is a sarcastic or bitter preference" (Longman 228). That is, under the sun it is better to be alive than dead, but not much.

[h]"Hence therefore the time and opportunity—perhaps also the desire—to make preparation. There is time to fix our interest in heaven—to live upon the real substantials to godliness" (Bridges 217).

[i]"Qoheleth is not moving from doubt to certainty but rather to urgency in the light of death" (Longman 229).

[j]Some commentators want to take the white clothes and anointing oil in a religious sense; however, the context seems to be indicating a festive, even frivolous frame of reference. Cf. Longman 230; Murphy 93.

[k]I cannot fail to comment on the irony and relevance, albeit unintended, of this idea to our contemporary world, where those who hold to an evolutionary framework extol time, chance and matter as the creative engines of all being. Solomon sees time and chance as destructive of all matter, including our own lives.

[l]The Hebrew verb has no definitive subjunctive form as, for example, Greek does. Instead the perfect may be employed to that end, as here. The subjunctive seems to be implied by the context, especially when verses 15 and 16 are taken together. The poor man had a good idea. Perhaps he was given an audience in private (v. 16), but he was summarily dismissed and forgotten. His idea could have saved the city, but vain and foolish rulers would not admit that wisdom could come from a peasant. See the margin note in NASB.

[m]This is a tragically personal note, for it was Solomon's foolishness that brought down the judgment of God against him, leading to the division of Israel into two nations and the ultimate dissolution of both. Prior to his death, Solomon was told that God was going to tear the nation apart because of him (1 Kings 11:9-13).

The Blessings of Common Sense: Ecclesiastes 10

[a]It is important to see this chapter in the context of the whole book; otherwise it looks like a somewhat distracted insertion of proverbs into what has been a profound essay on the meaning of life. I believe that Solomon is comparing all that he has been arguing to this point with everyday points of simple common sense that no one can gainsay. He seems to be saying that life in relationship to God makes as much sense as the most obvious matter of everyday wisdom. We can imagine the hearer nodding assent to everything Solomon says in these verses, reflecting in their light on all that he has been arguing to this point, rather like a lawyer who just before the peroration of his closing argument tells a homey tale to illustrate his case. In this light the chapter invites the reader to step down from the lofty heights of philosophical speculation into everyday experience and consider if what the author has been saying doesn't make as much sense as what everybody knows to be true, in the process providing a bit of comic relief before the closing arguments of the book.

[b]These eleven-plus lines are, of course, implied as introduction to this chapter.

[c]"Solomon does not refer to that trace of folly in a wise man or the lapses of the otherwise

good man; he instead refers to the tendency of folly to predominate over 'honorable wisdom'" (Kaiser 106). "It takes only a little of something bad to spoil something good" (Longman 239).

[d]Here Solomon builds on the image with which he concluded the preceding chapter, showing how such a prized commodity as wisdom is easily overshadowed by the foolishness of under-the-sun living.

[e]Right and left "were generally regarded in antiquity as indicating good and bad fortune respectively" (Whybray 151). "The right side is the side of prosperity and good fortune . . . and the left that of disaster and ill omen" (Murphy 101). Bridges gets the essence intended here: "Here it contrasts the wise man's ready prudence and circumspection with the fool's rashness and want of thoughtfulness" (Bridges 236).

[f]Hebrew "his heart is lacking."

[g]"The faithful adviser may be constrained to give unpalatable counsel; and the spirit of the ruler may rise up against him. Still let him not hastily leave the place" (Bridges 239).

[h]Hebrew "rich men." Solomon's point here seems to be that the prosperity of these men indicates their wisdom and suitability for rule.

[i]Hebrew "digs a pit." Commentators differ over whether this reference is to treachery or simple accident in the line of duty. As the verse paraphrase makes clear, I follow the former.

[j]"Wise men, unlike fools, take into their calculations the possible danger, and then they guard against it" (Kaiser 106).

[k]That is, who has enough common sense to sharpen his ax.

[l]Hebrew "to posses the tongue," that is, being able to charm snakes with one's voice. Some commentators see this as a parallel to the first part of the verse and translate it variously, for example, "there is no profit to a babbler." Babbling—the sign of a fool—is thus compared with ineptness in the snake charmer.

[m]Hebrew "multiplies words."

[n]Hebrew "he knows not to go to the city." This seems to imply that he cannot stop being a fool.

[o]What is suggested here is that from early morning such rulers are only concerned about filling their bellies—satisfying their sensual desires.

[p]Or so people think under the sun.

[q]I agree with Bridges that the intention of these proverbs is to strike at the reader's inner aptitudes and tendencies (Bridges 257). "The incompetence of the foolish is not rewarded with a lightning bolt of divine judgment, but with the steady decay of life's infrastructure" (Keddie 137).

[r]I follow Whybray in seeing Solomon's remark here as cynically intended (Whybray 156).

Make the Most of It—While You Can: Ecclesiastes 11

[a]This chapter is filled with irony. On the one hand Solomon offers sound advice,

consistent with what he has hitherto been saying about contentment, gratitude and diligence in life. On the other hand, his advice can be seen as the only hope that secular humans have for any happiness. "Make the most of the here and now," he seems to advise persons under the sun, "for it won't last long, and then you will be in torment forever." The chapter builds to the climax in verse 9, where Solomon places all life's activities under the judgment of God, whose assessment alone, at the end of our days, is all that matters. In the light of this, verse 10 is one final call to secular persons to stop fooling themselves and look at life in an eternal perspective, counsel that will be more definitively spelled out in chapter 12.

[b]Commentators seem to fall into one of two camps when it comes to the interpretation of verses 1 and 2. Some want to see them as recommending charitable acts, the giving of alms. Others are inclined, as I am, to take them as referencing prudence and industry in one's work and other opportunities. I find the overall drift of Ecclesiastes, and especially of this chapter, more amenable to this point of view. Keddie's remarks are especially helpful on this first verse.

[c]We might say, "Don't put all your eggs in one basket."

[d]As with investments, diversifying helps to ensure that a weakness or failure in one area will not destroy all one's wealth.

[e]The adversitive translation of the common conjunction seems to make more sense. Solomon is saying, "Read the signs, and make the most of your opportunities. But keep your limitations in mind."

[f]Hebrew "the one who keeps the wind."

[g]Alternately, some commentators want to see here a reference to the human spirit, since the Hebrew word for "wind" and "spirit" is the same. The implication is, as Paul puts it, that none of us can know what's going on in someone else's heart (1 Cor 2:11). The wind motif, however, seems to be more in keeping with the recurrent idea of chasing after the wind.

[h]Recall the legend of Icarus.

[i]One of the lessons of the parable of the talents (Mt 25:24-30).

[j]"Man prides himself upon what he knows, or fancies he knows—the extent of his knowledge. Much more reason has he to be humbled for the far wider extent of his ignorance" (Bridges 273). The point here seems to be that all persons must live by faith, since they cannot know everything and indeed hardly know much about many of the things they rely on for their daily lives. (How many of us really understand the inner workings of a computer, for instance, or the specific chemicals in our toothpaste?) So we trust in those who do—those who have made such things, are able to maintain them and assure us of their safety and usefulness—and follow the directions they give us. Solomon's point is that since all of life is like this, and therefore faith is required to successfully negotiate its many unknowns, does it not make sense, when it comes to life as a whole, to trust in the One who does know everything and maintains it continuously because he made it all?

ᵏThis little saying reminds us that Solomon is not a cynic about temporal existence. Although he seems at time to despair of its amounting to anything, this is strictly his under-the-sun perspective speaking. On the whole, he is positive about life and wants us to enjoy it as a gift from God, with proper gratitude and responsible stewardship.

ˡThat is, what we experience beyond the grave after a life of living under the sun.

ᵐHebrew "remove vexation from your heart"—"vexation" being whatever misleads, distracts or deceives us regarding the real meaning of life.

ⁿThat is, when they are devoted to merely secular living. See Solomon's conclusion in chapter 12.

ᵒSolomon "seems to be warning against not only the pitfalls of sin in the heart and in the flesh, but also false trust in youth and vigor that is so common in this world" (Keddie 152).

ᵖ"Yes, enjoy whatever you see or desire, but mark it down well and in the midst of your enjoyment remember that God will review even the quality of your pleasures and the manner in which you enjoy yourself" (Kaiser 117).

The Whole of a Person: Ecclesiastes 12

ᵃ"When he uses the word 'remember,' he is not asking for mere mental cognizance, for the biblical term 'remember' means much more than simple recall. Besides reflecting on and pondering the work of God in creating each individual and His world, there is the strong implication of action" (Kaiser 118).

ᵇVirtually every commentator sees the "strong men" as referring to the legs, which, I confess, puzzles me. When a young boy wants to flaunt his strength, he doesn't pull up his pant leg and show off his calves and thighs. He straightens his back, swells his chest and bulges his biceps. It makes sense to me to see this image as referring to the back and shoulders, although in the end it doesn't make any difference. What is intended is the notion of waning physical strength.

ᶜ"Such is the general picture of old age—in its gradual weakness of nature—decaying of sense—weakness of physical energy" (Bridges 288).

ᵈI admit that seeing the "grinding mill" as referring to the process of digestion is a novel interpretation. However, if the teeth, as part of the digestive system, are grinders and have already been alluded to, then this interpretation may not be far-fetched, especially given the problems with diet and digestion that often beset the elderly.

ᵉThis is the literal meaning of the Hebrew verb here, although textual critics suggest an emendation that can be translated "blossoms." This would then allow the almond tree to suggest the graying of hair. However, given the need to change the text, and the fact that the text as it stands can be readily understood, I see no need to follow this line of thinking. Cf. Longman 266 and Murphy 119.

ᶠThis Hebrew word is frequently rendered "caperberry" and refers to the fruit of the caper, which may have been considered an aphrodisiac. The translation as I have given it is equally valid and would seem to carry the same idea without limiting it to one specific area, that is, sexual desire.

[g]Many commentators want to see verses 8-14 as the work of a person different from Qoheleth, the worship leader or leader of the assembly, whom I have identified as Solomon. So widespread is this view that Whybray maintains that it is "universally agreed" (Whybray 169). However, I follow Kaiser and others in believing that this is not the case, but that the speaker simply shifts to a third-person perspective—as it is in the Hebrew, but which I have modified here—in order to emphasize the objectivity of his conclusion.

[h]The reference to the locust or grasshopper is traditionally taken to suggest the increasing difficulty the elderly have in merely getting around.

[i]Commentators generally want to see this as referring to a golden lamp hanging from a silver chain that breaks and falls to the floor. I think it has broader intimations.

[j]"The figure of the jar and pulley (v 6b) points to a well that has presumably been abandoned and is in disrepair. Fountain and life are combined many times in the Bible (Ps 36:9; Prov 10:11; 13:14). The water that symbolizes life can neither be drawn up from the well nor carried in a broken jar" (Murphy 120).

[k]"What then will happen to those who have lived and died without so much as a thought for God? It is unthinkable that they will possibly meet with his favour when they stand before him. The supreme folly of living as they have done will at last be revealed. All that they have ever lived for will have come to nothing. A life filled with a sense of futility will be followed by eternal disaster" (Olyott 68). Joyce Sutphen has captured the sense of this awareness in a poem that finds her taking issue with John Milton's contentedness, as one who knew the Lord, with his becoming blind and being willing and able to serve the Lord even in that state (see his sonnet "On His Blindness"). Her poem "Into Thin Air" appeared in the July 1999 issue of Poetry:

> The expense of spirit is, in fact, what
> I worry about. Not so much the body,
> dragging itself from limb to limb,
> falling helplessly down the vast
> recesses of night, hanging between
> dream and the uneven ticking of clocks.
>
> Not so much even the eyes failing, light
> spent, especially when I consider Degas,
> who had the weakest eyes in Paris,
> still managed to draw a black line around
> the body, shoulders edged with a perfection
> no one else, seeing better, could ever find.
>
> But who is it, I wonder, who also serves?
> And what is it to only stand and wait?

O body swayed and brightening glance,
cast off that waste of shame, and think
(beating mind!) of how it will be to fade
into thin air! What expense of spirit!

[l]"Solomon was supremely the wise man for Old Testament saints" (Kelley 146).

[m]Most translations and commentators render the Hebrew here as "words." However, the same word can mean "things" or "matters," and it would seem in the context of the whole book that such a rendering might work here. Solomon has already mentioned his attempt to keep his wisdom while indulging in worldly pleasures (2:9), only to see that wisdom undermined by folly. This verse would then serve as a summation of that point.

[n]First Kings 10.

[o]First Kings 4:32.

[p]That is, both wisdom itself and the ability to master wisdom in life come from one "Shepherd," whom Solomon intends us to understand is God. The shepherd's goad was used to move his flock ahead, while "well-driven nails" may refer to tent pegs securely fastened in the ground. Both are tools of the shepherd's work, just as the words and practice of wisdom are tools of God for accomplishing his purpose among human beings. The implication, of course, is that if we would have wisdom we must seek it from the Lord and not from a merely secular approach to life.

[q]To fear God means "having a reverent respect for him, because of his greatness and glory. To this is added gratitude for his kindness and mercy, awe at his power, confidence in his wisdom, submission to his will and delight in the experience of communing in him. Besides all this, the person who fears God has a deep affection for him, such as a child might have for a parent" (Olyott 66).

[r]Or "to be humankind." The word intends a generic meaning, not limited to one gender. "The general meaning of the statement is fairly clear: fearing God and obeying his commands is the most important thing a man or a woman can do" (Longman 282).

[s]"Not that the Preacher is an anti-intellect and therefore views books and learning as a waste of time, nor does he insist that we need our Bibles and nothing more. It is that man's learning and study has nothing to offer if they are not grounded in God's covenant word" (Kelley 147).